Searchlights for Spelling
Year 6 Teacher's Book

Chris Buckton   Pie Corbett

Contents

CAMBRIDGE
UNIVERSITY PRESS

CAMBRIDGE UNIVERSITY PRESS
Cambridge, New York, Melbourne, Madrid, Cape Town, Singapore,
São Paulo, Delhi, Dubai, Tokyo, Mexico City

Cambridge University Press
The Edinburgh Building, Cambridge CB2 8RU, UK

www.cambridge.org
Information on this title: www.cambridge.org/9780521891820

First published 2002
7th printing 2010

Printed in the United Kingdom by Short Run Press, Exeter

A catalogue record for this publication is available from the British Library

ISBN 978-0-521-89182-0 Paperback

ACKNOWLEDGEMENTS
Illustrations by Cecilia Johansson, Priscilla Lamont and Rachel Merriman.
Design and layout by Pentacor plc.

The publishers would like to thank the following for helping with the trialling of Searchlights for Spelling:

Abbotsmead Junior School, Cumbria
Ashbrook First School, Milton Keynes
Braniel Primary School, Belfast
High Bentham CP School, N. Yorks
Manorbrook Primary School, Bristol
St Richard's RC Primary School, Chichester
Watton-at-Stone Primary School, Herts

Barrow Community Learning Partnership (EAZ), Cumbria

Cover background photograph of coral reef: Kelvin Aitken/A.N.T./NHPA
(Natural History Photographic Agency)

Searchlights for Spelling

Searchlights for Spelling is a comprehensive spelling scheme for Years 2–6/Primary 3–7 that covers all the word-level spelling objectives of the National Literacy Strategy (NLS) and meets the requirements of the National Curriculum.

It is a systematic scheme for teaching the patterns of the English spelling system through stimulating, multi-sensory activities. It builds up spelling concepts through an investigative approach, equipping children with the skills to tackle new words as well as developing their strategies for the recall of key words and spelling patterns.

The scheme also builds on NLS programmes such as Progression in Phonics (PIPs) and Spelling Bank and is cross-referenced to them, making use of their basic interactive techniques such as 'Get Up and Go', 'Show Me', and 'Time Out' (see Key terms overleaf for further explanation).

Spelling for writing

The reason for learning to spell is to become fluent in everyday writing. *Searchlights* is designed to equip children to write fluently, rather than simply to learn and be tested upon decontextualised lists of words. It aims to make spelling enjoyable, through developing a sense of curiosity about words and an awareness of language patterns.

The sessions begin by deepening children's *understanding* of an objective or strategy, through direct teaching or investigation. This is followed by *applying* their understanding through shared writing and independent activities. It is important to ensure that spelling objectives are emphasised in the children's own writing, in order to reinforce the concept of spelling for a purpose.

A multi-sensory approach

The activities are based on four key learning styles:

- visual – remembering common patterns; writing words down to check whether they 'look' right; looking at the 'tricky' bit and trying the letters in a different order; looking for words within words; seeing the word in your mind, holding a word in your memory by seeing it, then looking to the top left of your mind to recall it.
- aural and oral – hearing and pronouncing words; emphasising or exaggerating pronunciation to aid learning (e.g. *Wed-nes-day*); breaking words into syllables or phonemes; remembering some words with a rhythmic strategy (e.g. *Mrs* d, *Mrs* i, *Mrs* ffi, *Mrs* c, *Mrs* u, *Mrs* lty: *difficulty*); using rhyme to spell by analogy.
- kinaesthetic – writing common patterns; tracing over words; sky-writing as you say each letter; getting the feel of common handwriting joins.
- cognitive – knowing rules, conventions, possible and impossible combinations; identifying word roots, suffixes and prefixes; using knowledge of grammar (e.g. *ed* – past tense), using mnemonics (e.g. *there is* a rat *in* sep arate).

By experiencing a multi-sensory teaching approach, children who learn in different ways have every chance of developing their ability to spell. Good spellers use a range of strategies. The whole-class and pupil activities in the scheme use a variety of approaches. To further support multi-sensory teaching, the above symbols are given next to the quickfire activities for each unit – Oddbods and Snip-snaps (see Key terms, page 4).

Identifying and representing phonemes

Searchlights generally follows the NLS conventions for identifying and representing phonemes, including the use of 'long' and 'short' to distinguish certain vowel phonemes. For the most part *Searchlights* adopts other NLS terminology. Phonemes are represented by bold type in all materials, while letter patterns are red in the Teacher's Book, OHTs and Pupil's Book and underlined in the Photocopy Masters Book.

It is important to note that the teaching of certain phonemes and their associated letter patterns can be affected by regional variation in pronunciation. You will need to adapt your teaching of these phonemes to suit the needs of your class. Such instances are noted in the relevant units.

Spelling practice – little and often

Children need frequent practice so that spelling becomes automatic and does not interfere with the act of composition. *Searchlights* is designed to be as flexible as possible and can be used in a variety of ways, depending on the needs of the children. The activities fit naturally into word-level work within the literacy hour and have a simple, regular pattern. They can be adapted for different classes and groups.

Spelling and handwriting

Searchlights emphasises the important link between spelling and handwriting, particularly in Year 6. Regular practice of handwriting joins helps to consolidate the learning of common letter strings. A joined script is offered wherever it is intended that a child will copy or continue writing.

Spelling log

It is helpful for children to develop the habit of keeping a personal spelling log. It can contain:

- collections of words arising from the independent activities;
- lists of oddbods (see Key terms below) and other 'tricky' words;
- results of spelling investigations;
- dictations and other tests;
- personal spelling targets;
- useful strategies or mnemonics;
- space for **Look Say Cover Write Check** practice.

A possible format for a spelling log is included in the Photocopy Masters Book for those who want to make use of it. Reference pages in the Pupil's Book and extra OHTs also provide useful material which the children could transfer to their log.

How to use *Searchlights for Spelling*

Key terms

Brush-ups:	activities which revisit objectives from the previous year, for those children who need more time to catch up.
Catch-you-out:	a word that is an exception to a specific rule or teaching point (e.g. where a word changes completely when forming a plural rather than just adding s or es).
Get Up and Go:	individual children come out to the front to demonstrate something.
Oddbod:	a 'tricky' word that causes common difficulties (featured on the top half of the OHT).
Time Out/ Show Me:	all children can respond by writing on dry-wipe boards and showing the spelling attempt.
Sky-writing:	drawing the shape of a letter or word in the air as an aid to memory.
Snip-snaps:	short, snappy ideas for further practice in applying the unit's objective or in learning key words.
Spelling log:	a personal ongoing record of words being learnt (see Photocopy Masters Book page 15).
Think about.../ Extra challenge:	both these suggestions take the children a little further in exploring or applying a spelling concept.

Colour-coding

Red type is used to highlight target letters and letter patterns, and to encourage children's own annotations. To highlight phonemes and distinguish them from spelling patterns, they are printed in bold type.

(In the Photocopy Masters Book, where colour is not used, letters and letter patterns are underlined and phonemes are in bold.)

The components

For each year there are four key components:

- ■ **Teacher's Book** – containing a double-page spread of step-by-step notes for each unit's teaching as well as background information.
- ■ **OHTs** (or Big Books for Years 2–4/Primary 3–5) – containing whole-class material for each unit as well as useful revision and supporting material.
- ■ **Pupil's Book** – containing a double-page spread of differentiated activities for each unit and reference pages with word lists and reminders of spelling rules and strategies.
- ■ **Photocopy Masters Book** – containing a photocopiable homework copymaster (PCM) for each unit as well as revision activities, assessment material and guidance for parents.

Together these resources provide 18 core units of work for the year (six units a term). Three additional units provide further material, which can be fitted in as necessary.

Each unit comprises two parts:

- ■ Part 1 – introduces spelling objective(s).
- ■ Part 2 – takes the objective(s) one step further, or introduces a further objective, and provides a test dictation.

Part 1

Teaching the objective(s): Swift, lively interactive teaching of objective(s), using the Overhead Transparencies, plus teaching of key words, including 'oddbods' (see Key terms).

Using the objective(s): Developing the skill or concept through writing, including brief opportunities for shared writing.

Independent work (Pupil's Book): Differentiated activities focusing on reinforcement and extension of target objectives (see Differentiation, opposite). This may take place as part of a literacy hour, or at another time.

Review (plenary): Review of independent work and recap of main teaching points.

Homework: Reinforcement task, with investigative element which can involve other family members; Words to Learn for the unit's dictation.

Part 2

An extended whole-class session.

Teaching the objective(s): Usually revisiting and developing the unit focus, using the bottom half of the OHT.

Using the objective(s): Writing with the class, pausing and discussing spelling points.

Review (plenary): Review and summary of new learning, and discussion of homework findings.

Follow-up homework: This allows for further exploration or reinforcement of learning.

Test dictation: Class dictation that includes examples of the spelling objective and oddbod(s) for the week.

Differentiation

Independent activities in the Pupil's Book are differentiated at three levels, A, B and C. A and B activities consolidate children's learning of the key objectives of the unit, while C activities are more challenging or address a further objective. C activities may anticipate Part 2. Children could work through all three when appropriate. The Extra challenge in some units extends children's learning further.

Children who find spelling particularly difficult may need extra time to revisit key objectives from the previous year or years. For Year 6/Primary 7 children who need extra phonics teaching, use activities for the earlier steps in the NLS Progression in Phonics (PiPs). *Searchlights* also provides a bank of Brush-up ideas based on the previous year's objectives as well as four extra revision PCMs.

For each unit, the Words to Learn list on the homework PCM is differentiated (A, B, C) so that some children can be given fewer target words to learn.

Paired spelling

Children could spend ten minutes every day following this simple procedure in order to learn their individual lists (between five and 18 words at a time). This procedure could also be introduced to parents and it is given as part of the 'How to help your child with spelling' guidance (see the Photocopy Masters Book, pages 47–48).

- The child reads the word; says it aloud; spells the letters out; tries to spell it out without looking.
- Together, parent/partner and child discuss 'tricky bits' and devise a way of remembering them.
- If the child finds the word hard to remember, repeat the first two stages as necessary before attempting to write.
- The spelling partner/parent covers the word.
- The child writes it down.
- Together they check – if incorrect, revisit two or three more times.

Assessment

The units include a dictation test as well as a termly SATs-type test to track progress. The 20 words selected for each SATs test (pages 11–14 of the Photocopy Masters Book) focus on the term's objectives as well as key words or oddbods, or both. The first underlined word in each test is for practice before you start. See the notes in the English Tests Teacher's Guide (QCA) for more guidance on how to give the test.

To be useful, spelling tests should always be diagnostic. Look carefully at the results to find out what strategies the children are using. It is important, too, not to penalise them for incorrect but intelligent, plausible guesses. One useful approach is to allocate two marks to each word: the first mark could be given if the target phoneme, pattern or rule is correct (e.g. ai spelt correctly in r*ai*n) and the second if the whole word is correct.

A simple Tracking sheet to help you monitor children's progress is provided in the Photocopy Masters Book (page 3). Children's involvement in assessing their own progress in spelling is very important. To encourage children to review their own learning, yearly self-assessment sheets with 'I can' targets are also provided (see Photocopy Masters Book, page 16).

Test dictation

The object of regular dictation is to give the children practice in spelling words in context, reinforcing the importance of accurate spelling in writing.

Searchlights dictation provides three levels of differentiated sentences for each unit. The children learn the words before they are tested on some of them in context. In Year 6/Primary 7 there are

18 words to learn per unit: comprising words related to the unit's objective(s); and wherever possible words are drawn from the NLS list of high frequency words); and the oddbod(s).

Test scores and comments can be recorded on the teacher Tracking sheet (see Photocopy Masters Book pages 3–5). The suggested procedure for the test dictation is as follows.

Introduction (first unit)
- Explain to the children what a dictation is.
- Tell them that you will be dictating sentences.

Procedure
- Tell them that first, you'll read the whole sentence while they listen. Specify whether you want them to write out the whole sentence or just the target word.
- Then explain that you'll read a little bit at a time while they write it down (if they are writing out the whole sentence).
- Tell them what to do if they come to a word they don't know: try to break the word up into its sounds, or think of another rhyming word which perhaps they can remember how to spell.
- Give prompts where appropriate, e.g. reminding them of rules or asking questions such as: *Remember that oddbod? Listen to that word again – what sound can you hear?*
- Read the passage through again so that they can check their writing.
- Note: Make sure that you do not expose strugglers. Children should simply write the words they have learnt (A, A/B, A/B/C). There is no need to draw attention to difference here.

Homework

For each unit, a homework PCM provides the related list of words to learn for the dictation test and a task that reinforces the unit's teaching, or focuses on revision. The sheets also encourage an investigative approach. Words to Learn for each unit are offered in three levels of difficulty. They are referred to as key words in the Photocopy Masters Book and listed there in full on pages 6–7.

Parents/carers are offered further guidance on a separate PCM: 'How to help your child with spelling'.

Scope and sequence chart – Year 6

Unit	NLS Objectives	OHT	Pupil's Book	Homework PCM	Snip-snaps	Oddbods
1 Long words – unstressed vowels 1	NLS 6.1.W4	Stressed and unstressed syllables	Identifying stressed and unstressed syllables and vowels Working out spelling strategies	Finding ways to remember	Unstressed Vowel Over-pronounce Word Focus	conclusion
2 Word roots, prefixes and suffixes	NLS 6.1.W5	Prefixes and suffixes Working out meanings	Matching prefixes and suffixes to meanings Making words with prefixes and suffixes	Alien affixes	Prefixes New Words Key Words	peaceful
3 Connectives	NLS 6.1.W3, W6	Identifying connectives	Making and spelling connectives	The meanwhile poem	wh Words Meanings Early	other
4 Old and new words	NLS 6.1.W7, W8, W9	Meanings of Old English words	Investigating Old English words	Kennings	Greek Words Words from Names Latin Words	chocolate
5 Spelling rules 1	NLS 6.1.W1, W2, W3	Spelling rules	Looking for patterns in words with 'hard' and 'soft' c and g	Is it really i before e?	Gee Up! qu Words Word Focus	weight
6 Spelling rules 2	NLS 6.1.W1, W2, W3	Suffixes able, ible and ion	Adding suffixes with able or ible	able and ible	Adding ly ct or ed? Doobeedoo!	queue
7 Long words – unstressed vowels 2	NLS 6.2.W4	Words with unstressed vowels	Identifying unstressed vowels and working out spelling strategies	More ways to remember	Bag of Tricks al Words Settle	definite
8 Words for argument	NLS 6.2.W1, W3, W8	Related words for argument	Finding related words and spelling strategies	Wh words	Dominoes Believe It or Not wh and the Words	argument
9 Spelling rules and mnemonics	NLS 6.2.W1, W2, W3, W4	Spelling aids	Using rhymes, rules and mnemonics	Time for a rhyme	Mnemonic Word Chant Rainbow	embarrass
10 Spelling rules and strategies 1	NLS 6.2.W1, W2, W3, W4	Consonant doubling and suffixes	Investigating consonant doubling	Double trouble	Hissing Plurals Plurals Which One?	beginning
11 Word origins	NLS 6.2. W2, W3, W4, W5	Words with Greek and Latin roots	Finding meanings of Greek and Latin roots	Words with Greek roots	French Words Indian Words Arabic Words	technology
12 Revisiting suffixes and prefixes	NLS 6.2. W1, W2, W3, W4, W5	Meanings of prefixes and suffixes	Using prefixes to create opposites Investigating prefixes and suffixes	Making choices	Common Errors Mis-spellings Roots	skilful

Scope and sequence chart – Year 6 cont.

Unit	NLS Objectives	OHT	Pupil's Book	Homework PCM	Snip-snaps	Oddbods
13 Confusables	NLS 6.3.W3, W4	Homophones	Identifying and using homophones and easily confused words	Off, of and have	Homophone Riddles Homophones Topsy-turvy	advise advice
14 Spelling rules and strategies 2	NLS 6.3.W2, W3, W4	'Long' vowel sounds	Identifying words with 'long' vowel sounds sounds **ai, ee, oo, ie, oa**	Word sort	Reveal Impossible Endings Quickfire Spelling	although
15 Spelling of dialect and memory joggers	NLS 6.3.W1, W3, W4	Dialect spelling Memory aids	Correcting spellings Inventing mnemonics	Captain Kidd	Which One? Confusables Right or Wrong?	questionnaire
16 Sound and spelling patterns plus silent letters	NLS 6.3.W2, W4	Sound and spelling patterns Silent consonants	Spelling words related by spelling pattern or meaning	**Sort the sound**	Beat the Clock Picture It **gh** Wipe-off	diamond
17 Word play	NLS 6.3.W6, W7	Riddles and puns Spoonerisms	Solving and inventing anagrams	**Con** puzzle	Collective Nouns Alliteration Anagrams	consequence
18 Word games	NLS 6.3.W5, W6, W7	Making new words Word game	Inventing new words	Hide and seek words	Rhyme Quickfire Adverbs	outrageous
Additional 1 Prefixes and suffixes	NLS 6.1.W5	Prefixes, suffixes and roots	Using prefixes to make opposites	Testing the rule	Break It Up! Roots Odd Plurals	sincerely
Additional 2 Spelling strategies and common words	NLS 6.2.W2, W3, W4	Memory aids	Finding ways of remembering spellings Filling in the missing letters	Wordsearch	Compounds Plurals Adding **ed** and **ing**	sequence
Additional 3 Word play and spelling check-up	NLS 6.3.W6	Riddles Word play	Writing riddles and acrostics	Spelling check up	Reveal/Which One? I Spy Dominoes	encyclopedia

YEAR	TEACHER RESOURCE	WHOLE-CLASS TEACHING	PUPIL RESOURCE	HOMEWORK REINFORCEMENT ASSESSMENT
Y2	Teacher's Book	Big Book	Pupil's Book	Copymasters
Y3	Teacher's Book	Big Book	Pupil's Book	Copymasters
Y4	Teacher's Book	Big Book	Pupil's Book	Copymasters
Y5	Teacher's Book	OHTs	Pupil's Book	Copymasters
Y6	Teacher's Book	OHTs	Pupil's Book	Copymasters

Long words – unstressed vowels 1

Objective for Unit 1

To spell unstressed vowels in polysyllabic words

Part 1 | **You need** OHT 1; dry-wipe boards or notebooks; Pupil's Book pages 2–3; PCM 1

Whole class
- Together, sound out a word where all the vowels are easily heard, e.g. *Friday*. Remind children that some vowels are hard to hear because they are spoken either quickly or quietly – they are 'unstressed', e.g. we do not say 'read-er', but say the second vowel quietly: 'read-uh'.
- Focus on the top half of the OHT and read the words.
- Ask the children to write the words on dry-wipe boards, showing the syllable breaks and then to underline the stressed syllables.
- Show Me: check the children's efforts; you mark the breaks and syllables on the OHT. (<u>par</u>/a/llel, con/<u>serv</u>/a/tory, <u>lem</u>/on/<u>ade</u>, <u>con</u>/son/ant, tre/<u>mend</u>/ous, fan/<u>tas</u>/tic)
- On which syllable does the stress most often fall?
- Say each word out loud and highlight the tricky unstressed vowels in another colour.
- Discuss ways of remembering spellings of words with unstressed syllables, e.g.
  - Over-pronounce the unstressed vowel ('*a-stron-o-mi*').
  - Highlight words within words (*skel<u>et</u>on*).
  - Make up a mnemonic (*misers are miserable*).
- Introduce the oddbod: *conclusion* – see below.

Pupil activities

A: Identify stressed syllables and find out which vowel appears most often in unstressed syllables.

B and C: Identify stressed vowels and invent ways to remember spellings.

Extra challenge: investigate words which contain different pronunciations of the same letter.

Review
- Ask children to list ways of remembering how to tackle unstressed vowels: try saying it as it might sound if the vowel was clear; linking it to other words in the same family finding words within words; making up a mnemonic.
- Recap which vowels are most common in unstressed syllables. (a, e, o).

Homework

Identify stressed syllables and invent mnemonics.

Oddbod conclusion
- Identify the prefix, which is easy to spell. What other words use this prefix? (**con**nect, **con**tain, **con**firm, etc).
- List other similar verbs, e.g. *include, decide, collide, provide*.
- Turn these into nouns and see what happens to the spelling, e.g. *inclusion, decision, collision, provision*.
- Generalise a rule, e.g. polysyllabic verbs ending in de drop these letters and add sion, e.g. *conclude – conclusion*.

Snip-snap Unstressed Vowel
- Say a word that has an unstressed vowel, e.g. *holiday, lettuce, signature, journalist, faithfully, together, again*.
- Together, break the word into syllables. You draw a line on the board for each syllable.
- Get Up and Go: ask volunteers to come and fill in a syllable they think they can spell.
- Discuss different tactics for remembering or working out the spellings.

NLS objective for Unit 1
6.1.W4

Part 2 | You need   OHT 1; dry-wipe boards or notebooks

Whole class
- Focus on the bottom half of the OHT. Explain that in some words we write more syllables than we pronounce.
- Read each pair of words aloud together.
- Make sure that the children can distinguish between words with unstressed (but still pronounced) vowels and words with unpronounced vowels (e.g. the middle vowel in *interest*).
- Ask the children to divide each word into segments and underline the tricky bit (the unstressed vowel) in each.
- Encourage them to work out ways to remember how to spell each word, calling upon all the possible strategies, e.g.:
  - over-pronouncing;
  - words within words;
  - related words;
  - mnemonics.
- Invent sentences that use these words, e.g. *I tried to <u>describe</u> what a vowel and a <u>consonant</u> were but failed!*

Review
- Look at the icons on the inside back cover of the Pupil's Book. Ask children which of their senses they can use to help them remember how to spell words with unstressed vowels.

- Homework review.
- Share ways of remembering the words.

Follow-up homework
- Ask the children to think of other words that have unstressed or unpronounced vowels or consonants.

Test dictation
OB Half-way through the film, Dan guessed the conclusion.
A   At our last barbecue, a mosquito fell in my lemonade.
     The Internet is a real benefit when I'm doing my homework.
B   Dad felt nervous for a week after he found the skeleton in the garage.
     The journalist bravely set off on her mission to write about the war.
C   Mice and rabbits love to eat lettuce and carrots, but I don't!

Snip-snap Over-pronounce
- You say a word that has an unstressed vowel but over-pronounce it to make the spelling memorable, e.g. 'sig-na-ture', 'gram-mar', 'mar-ga-rine'.
- Children repeat the over-pronunciations and then write the spellings down on dry-wipe boards.

Snip-snap Word Focus
- How can you remember the word *quiet*?
  - u *and* i *should be* quiet.
  - Chant 'u-i-e *before* tea'.
  - q *is always followed by* u.

Word roots, prefixes and suffixes

Objective for Unit 2

To use word roots, prefixes and suffixes to help spelling

Part 1 | **You need**   OHT 2; dry-wipe boards or notebooks; Pupil's Book pages 4–5; PCM 2

Whole class
- Focus on the top half of the OHT and look at the example retrainable. Focus on the meaning of the prefix re (again) and the suffix able (can be).
- Read the root words in the second column. Invite the children to make up new words on dry-wipe boards by adding suitable prefixes and suffixes to the root words.
- Show Me: children show their new words as you work through the chart. Check spellings as you go.
- Discuss prefix and suffix meanings as you tackle each new prefix–root–suffix combination.
- Discuss how adding the prefix or suffix changes the meaning of the word root. Point out that suffixes in particular often change the word class as well (e.g. less changes nouns to adjectives).
- Write up sentences using common prefixes and suffixes and discuss spellings, e.g. *A triathlete has the misfortune of retraining for three different events. He photographed the transcription with his microscopic supercamera.*
- Introduce the oddbod: *peaceful* – see below.

Pupil activities
A: Match prefixes and suffixes to their meanings and combine with word roots.
B: Deduce what prefixes and suffixes mean.
C: Link parts of words together to form new words.

Think about ...: Look at suffixes, prefixes, word roots to help with spelling.

Review
- Ask children to tell you which prefixes have the following meanings: 'small' (micro), 'two' (bi), 'wrongly' (mis), 'again' (re), 'less than' (sub).

Homework
Match prefixes and suffixes to word roots.

Oddbod   peaceful
- Break the word into its two parts – *peace* and *full* (meaning full of peace).
- Look for words within the word, e.g. *pea, ace*.
- Invent a mnemonic, e.g. *Aces and peas are peaceful!*
- Chant the letters rhythmically then speedwrite the word on dry-wipe boards.
- Remember the rule that *full* becomes ful as a suffix.

Snip-snap   Prefixes
- Write up a list of common prefixes, e.g. ex, in, duo, inter, con, bi, micro, tele, hydro/hydra, sub.
- In pairs, on dry-wipe boards, spell real or invented words using these prefixes and word roots such as *board, correct, national, cycle, film, phone, way, human, vision, scope, junction, light, plane, tribute, lateral.*

NLS objectives for Unit 2

6.1.W5

Part 2 | **You need**   OHT 2

Whole class ■ Recap the key points:
- ■ prefixes are added to the front of words;
- ■ suffixes are added to the end of words;
- ■ both change meaning of the word root but suffixes can also change the word class.

■ Focus on the bottom half of the OHT and ask the children to work in pairs, identifying the two prefixes and two suffixes. Tell them to discuss what they might mean and then write their ideas down on dry-wipe boards.

■ Check ideas and meanings: mis ('wrong' or 'wrongly'), super ('great' or 'more than'), ous ('having' or 'being like'), ful ('full of' or 'the amount that can be held by something').

■ Show Me: ask the children to list other words that use the same prefixes or suffixes.

■ Demonstrate writing sentences using common prefixes and suffixes, discussing spelling, e.g. *Superman's famous partner was punished for misconduct.*
A spoonful of sugar helps the monstrous medicine go down. Point out again that in the cases of ous and ful, the word class of the root is also changed (noun to adjective).

Review ■ Ask what happens when you add the suffix less to a word (nouns change to adjectives). What other suffixes do the same thing? (ful, ous) What does the suffix able do? (changes verbs to adjectives)

■ Homework review.

■ When spelling a word, it helps to think about whether it has a suffix or prefix. Think of other words that share the same features.

Follow-up homework ■ Collect and list other common prefixes and suffixes. Use a dictionary to find their meanings.

Test dictation OB Having a sauna is a very peaceful activity.
A   In February there were subzero temperatures everywhere.
I had a spoonful of raspberry sauce on my ice-cream.
B   You can book international and transatlantic flights through an agency.
The museum of prehistoric art isn't as boring as you might think.
C   Famous cinema actors sometimes misbehave at parties.

Snip-snap   New Words
- ■ Write up a list of suffixes: ing, able, ive, ion, or, ent.
- ■ Say one of the following words: *invent, depend, bear, construct.*
- ■ In pairs, on dry-wipe boards, children use that word to make new words by adding the suffixes.

Snip-snap   Key Words   👁 🗩
- ■ Write up *bring, brought* and *buy, bought.* Use different colours to distinguish the tenses.
- ■ Say some sentences aloud, e.g. *I went to the shop and* bought *a banana. I've* brought *my homework to school.*
- ■ Children put thumbs up if the word should have an r and thumbs down for no r.

3 Connectives

Objective for Unit 3

To use spelling strategies and to spell and understand connectives

Part 1 | You need

OHT 3; dry-wipe boards or notebooks; Pupil's Book pages 6–7; PCM 3

Whole class
- Focus on the top half of the OHT and read the passage together.
- Invite children to underline the connectives and make a list of these words for future use in their writing.
- Brainstorm other connectives and add them to the list.
- Discuss different strategies for spelling the connectives, e.g.
  - building up spellings by syllabic parts;
  - using prefixes, suffixes and common letter strings;
  - applying knowledge of any relevant rules and exceptions;
  - building words from related words;
  - using mnemonics;
  - using visual clues to double check – does it look right?
- Use the list of connectives, continue the passage, e.g.
  Moreover, I was chosen to play for the school team, so I settled in quite happily in the end!
- Introduce the oddbod: *other* – see below.

Pupil activities
A: Work out ways to remember spellings of connectives.
B: Build connectives from roots or parts.
C: Use a pattern of connectives to write a poem.

Think about ...: Use of the comma in sentences that start with a connective.

Review
- Recap: connectives are words or phrases that help link ideas together. They can be used to link one sentence to another or to extend a sentence. Ask children to list some connectives on their dry-wipe boards.
- Connectives require a range of different spelling strategies because they do not fall into any one category. Ask children to share some of the strategies they have found.

Homework
Continue a poem, spelling the connective correctly.

Oddbod   other
- Children think of rhymes for *other* (e.g. *mother, brother, smother*) and write them on dry-wipe boards to show.
- Draw attention to the within other by using two colours.

Snip-snap   wh Words
- Write up connectives based on wh words, e.g. *whereas, whenever, when, while, whilst, whatever, whoever.*
- Ask children how they can remember the words (they are all made out of two separate words).
- Make up mnemonics to help you remember *while* and *whilst*, e.g. White horses in large earrings; Why has Isabel lost Sam's toy?)

NLS objectives for Unit 3

6.1.W3   6.1.W6

Part 2 | You need   OHT 3; children's own reading books; dry-wipe boards or notebooks

Whole class
- Focus on the bottom half of the OHT and read through the instruction and the words.
- Classify the connectives according to the job they do within a text. (*Grammar for Writing*, page 187 is helpful on this point.)
- Once the words have been assigned to the correct category, take time to look at the spellings.
- Show Me: cover the words one at a time and invite the children to spell each one on a dry-wipe board.
- Try to add a new word to each category, e.g. *furthermore, on the other hand, in other words, as a result, later.*
- Try to add a new category, e.g. listing (*firstly, finally*) or reinforcing (*besides, anyway*).
- Ask the children to work in pairs to search through their books and jot down further examples of connectives that fall into these categories.

Review
- Look at the lists of connectives you made in the whole-class session. Ask children to suggest sentences, each including one connective, and to practise writing the connectives on their dry-wipe boards.

- Homework review.
- Ask the children to continue the poem, using a variety of connectives.

Follow-up homework
- Keep checklists of connectives for different types of writing, to be used for future reference.

Test dictation
OB That other girl's blue sari is very similar to my sister's.
A   You should read this leaflet before you set up your new computer.
       I haven't seen a lioness since my safari holiday last year.
B   Wherever I go, my loyal dog always waits faithfully nearby.
       While doing the difficult multiplication, I made a bad miscalculation.
C   The sea was treacherous, but nonetheless the little boat made it safely to the quay.

Snip-snap   Meanings
- Write up the compound words: *furthermore, henceforward, notwithstanding, whenever, nonetheless.*
- Children try to work out meaning of each word by splitting it into parts, putting the meanings of the parts together, and thinking about the way it is used.
- Working in pairs, they jot down possible definitions.

Snip-snap   Early
- To remember the word *early*, use the mnemonic: *There's an ear in early.*
- Children practise speedwriting the word, then try writing with their eyes closed. It may help them to 'take a picture' of the word first.
- Discuss how to spell other words from early, e.g. *earliness* (note that the y changes to i), *earlier, earliest.*

4 Old and new words

Objective for Unit 4

To investigate how spelling and language change over time

Part 1

You need OHT 4; dry-wipe boards or notebooks; Pupil's Book pages 8–9; PCM 4

Whole class

- Focus on the top half of the OHT. Explain that the extract is from *A Midsummer Night's Dream*, written in the late 1500s.
- Read it through together. Investigate how the spelling has changed: take it line by line and ask children to guess the equivalent modern-day words, writing on dry-wipe boards. Rough translation: *Have you got the flower there? / Welcome, traveller. / Yes, there it is. / Please give it to me. / I know a bank…*
- Explain that *hast thou*, *ay* and *pray thee* are Old English, sometimes called 'archaic' words. Do the children know other archaic words?
- Discuss why words change (e.g. due to the influence of foreign exploration or travel) or fall out of use (e.g. patterns of speech change, the reason for using a word no longer exists) and why we need new words (e.g. for new technology).
- Together, write a list of computer vocabulary and check spellings, e.g. *computer, disk, e-mail, megabyte, RAM, desktop, program, icon, Internet, Web, hypertext, software, hardware, format, online*. Use some of these to write simple definitions, e.g. *E-mail is a method of sending a message electronically from one computer to another.*
- Introduce the oddbod: *chocolate* – see below.

Pupil activities

A: Investigate words in an extract from an archaic ballad.
B: Investigate words from a Spenser extract (1500s).
C: Investigate words from a Caxton extract (1490). (Answer: … *written in old English, to be translated into the English we use today. It certainly was written in such a way that it was more like Dutch than English; I couldn't make it understandable.*)

Extra challenge: Investigate months of the year.

Review

- Recap: over time, the spellings of words and word usage change.
- Discuss new words currently used in the children's language (with care!) Which words do they think might fall out of use in the next 50–100 years? (e.g. *cassette recorder, typewriter*)

Homework Match modern invented terms to their meanings.

Oddbod chocolate ⒥ ⊖ ◎ ⌇

- Say the word slowly as it is spelled, breaking it into syllables – '*choc-o-late*'.
- The middle and end are easy, Chant '*never be late / for choc-o-late*'.
- The opening ch is easy.
- Write up *chockolate* and *chocolate* – which looks correct? Remember that *chocolate* is made from *cocoa* to help with the spelling.

Snip-snap Greek Words ⌇

- These words or parts of words come from Greek: *bio* (Gr. *bios* – 'life'), *therm* (Gr. *therme* – 'heat'), *phobia* (Gr. *phobos* – 'fear'), *photo* (Gr. *phos* – *photos*, 'light'), *astro* (Gr. *astron* – 'star'), *graph* (Gr. *graphein* – 'to write'), *phon* (Gr. *phone* – 'voice').
- Say a root and ask the children to spell a word containing it.

NLS objectives for Unit 4

6.1.W7   6.1.W8   6.1.W9

Part 2 | You need   OHT 4; dry-wipe boards or notebooks

Whole class
- Focus on the bottom half of the OHT and explain that this is an extract from a poem written by Chaucer in the 1300s.
- Read it together and note changes in spellings from Chaucer's time to our own. Ask children to guess the meanings of words, writing on dry-wipe boards and showing suggestions. Rough translation:
  A thousand times I've heard people say
  That there is joy in heaven and pain in hell,
  And I believe that that is so;
  But, nonetheless, I also know well
  That there's no-one living in this country
  Who has been in either heaven or hell.
- Explain that many words we use every day are from other languages although sometimes we do not realise it. Point out that many of these are words for food, e.g. *pizza* (Italian), *curry* (Tamil), *kebab* (Arabic), *chocolate* (Nahuatl, an Aztec language).

Review
- Recap: over time, the spellings and meanings of words alter. Modern English has many words from other languages. Knowing their origins may help in remembering their spellings.
- Ask children to think of some words for food (or musical terms) which come from Italian (e.g. *pizza*, *pasta*, *spaghetti*, *macaroni*). Which letters appear most often at the ends of these words?

- Homework review.
- Summarise what is known about kennings.

Follow-up homework
- Make a list of archaic words or everyday English words from other languages. Ask your friends or family to help.

Test dictation
- OB Ben made a chocolate and raspberry cake for his mother's birthday.
- A   I saved my work onto my computer's hard disk.
      E-mail is a really quick way of writing to your friends.
- B   In biology we used a thermometer to see how hot it was.
      Dad was reading a biography of his favourite Russian film star.
- C   Yoghurt is a low fat food, therefore it is good for you.
      Jill ate a big tomato and banana sandwich for lunch.

Snip-snap Words from Names
- Ask children to think of words for everyday things that are named after people. Give examples to start them off, e.g. *sandwich* (after the Earl of Sandwich), *wellington* (after the Duke of Wellington), *biro* (after its inventor, the Hungarian Ladislao Biró).

Snip-snap Latin Words
- Write up a Latin root, e.g. aqua (water), urbs (town), ambulare (to walk), octo (eight).
- On dry-wipe boards, children write down as many words as they can think of, based on that root.

5 Spelling rules 1

Objective for Unit 5

To apply knowledge of spellings, rules and exceptions

Part 1 | You need
OHT 5; dry-wipe boards or notebooks; Pupil's Book pages 10–11; PCM 5

Whole class

- Focus on the top half of the OHT. Read the words in the first line and ask the children what sound the ie and ei vowels make. Can anyone explain the rule? (See Review.) Ask the children to add further words to see whether the rule holds good.
- Talk about the catch-you-outs: the most common exceptions are *weird*, *seize*, *species*; proper names, e.g. *Keith*, *Sheila*; words that make an **ay** sound such as *weigh*, *sleigh*, *neigh*.
- Read the words in the second and third lines, emphasising the 'hard' and 'soft' c and g. Ask whether anyone can identify the spelling pattern or rule. (See Review.)
- Talk about the catch-you-outs: *Celtic* can be pronounced either way and *geese* has a 'hard' g. The word *gill* has a 'hard' g but the girl's name *Gillian* has a 'soft' g.
- Write a few silly sentences using some of the spellings, e.g. *The thief intended to deceive. The cockerel rode on his cycle to the cinema. A gaggle of geese wearing goggles giggled at Ginger.* (*geese* and *giggled* are both catch-you-outs.)
- Introduce the oddbod: *weight* – see below.

Pupil activities

A: Sort words with 'soft' and 'hard' c.
B: Identify patterns in the occurrence of soft and hard g.
C: Identify patterns in the occurrence of soft and hard c.

Think about ...: Catch-you-outs with a 'hard' g.

Review

- Recap the spelling rules with the whole class:
- i before e when it sounds like a 'long' **ee**, except after c.
- c usually makes a 'soft' sound when followed by e, i and y; it makes a 'hard' sound when followed by a, o and u.
- g is much less reliable than c at softening (see Part 2).
- Ask children to remind you of the catch-you-outs which don't follow the 'i before e except after c' rule.

Homework

Test the 'i before e' rule on a list of common words.

Oddbod   weight

- Approach this word by building it up bit by bit.
- Write down first and last letters (the easy bits) leaving a space in between: w_____t.
- Remember you can add *eight* to w to get *weight*. Use two colours to show the word *eight* within *weight*.
- Chant a mnemonic for ight words: *iguanas go home tonight*. Then fill in the we.

Snip-snap   Gee Up!

- Say words with a ge or dge ending. Use: *wedge*, *ledge*, *hedge*, *badge*, *cage*, *rage*, *page*, *fudge*, *nudge*, *binge*, *fringe*. Children write the words on dry-wipe boards. Score one point for each correct answer.
- Ask children to generalise a rule: e.g. use ge after a 'long' vowel and dge after a 'short' vowel.
- Then ask them to write the Indian word *raj*. It's a catch-you-out – no English word ends in j.

<table>
<tr><td colspan="3">NLS objectives for Unit 5</td></tr>
<tr><td>6.1.W1</td><td>6.1.W2</td><td>6.1.W3</td></tr>
</table>

Part 2 | You need   OHT 5; dry-wipe boards or notebooks

Whole class
- Focus on the bottom half of the OHT and read the instruction.
- Add ge, gi or gy to each word with children giving suggestions on dry-wipe boards.
- Ask the children to suggest a rule. What is the effect of e and i? What do they notice about the occurrence of y?
- Look at *guilty*. What does the u do? Are there other words like this? (*guillotine, guild, guitar*)
- Invite the children to write some more phrases using these letter combinations on the board for others to complete.

Review
- g is less easy to predict than c.
- y, e and o usually soften the g.
- u and a usually harden the g .
- i can work either way!
- Ask children to suggest examples for each of these rules.

- Homework review.
- In groups or pairs, children compare the 'friend' spelling aids. Which one do they think works best?

Follow-up homework
- List the rules covered. Remember, you are better off having a rule to follow and then trying to learn the exceptions, than having no rule at all!

Test dictation
OB   Bob ate nothing but yoghurt for a week as he wanted to lose weight.
A   Sally loves exploring the Internet whenever she can.
     I have wanted to be an astronaut since I was eight.
B   Bill tried to stay calm although he had a phobia of flying.
     Today I'm going to browse through those boxes of old toys in the cellar.
C   The footballer missed an easy goal owing to a miscalculation.

Snip-snap   qu Words
- Put children into groups of four or five.
- Within each group, children take it in turns to say a qu word and write it on a dry-wipe board.
- The group with the longest list of correctly spelt words is the winner. Deduct a point for any mis-spellings.
- What do they notice about the spelling of these words? Ask the groups to generalise a rule with two points to it, e.g. q is always followed by u and at least one other vowel.

Snip-snap   Word Focus
- Give pairs or groups of children 18 of the key words from PCM 5 (not no/know).
- Ask them to sort the words into sets according to their spelling rules.
- Other pairs or groups try and guess what criteria was used.

6 Spelling rules 2

Objective for Unit 6

To apply knowledge of spelling rules and exceptions

Part 1

You need OHT 6; dry-wipe boards or notebooks; Pupil's Book pages 12–13; PCM 6

Whole class
- Focus on the top half of the OHT and read the words together.
- Show Me: children write spellings on dry-wipe boards, adding able or ible. (*lovable, valuable, changeable, affordable, noticeable, forcible, reducible*)
- To which word class do able and ible words belong? (adjectives)
- Talk about the occurrence of these endings: able is most common; words that end in an **s** sound usually end in ible. Where the base word is not altered, usually add able (note that *visible* and *possible* do not have an obvious root like the other words). Test these ideas by spelling other similar words (*reliable, readable, avoidable, sensible, responsible, terrible*). Use a dictionary to check, if the children are unsure. Exaggerating the ending can help, e.g. '*invis-ible*'.
- Use some of these words to write a few sentences, e.g. *The lovable, affordable dog became invisible.*
- Introduce the oddbod: *queue* – see below.

Pupil activities

A: Take off the suffix and spell the word root. Write sentences to explore meanings.

B: Add ible or able to words that end in ion and explore changes in word class.

C: Decide whether words ending in a 'hard' c or g take able or ible and use such words in a written description.

Extra challenge: Do words ending in the letter patterns nse or nce take able or ible?

Review
- Selecting ible or able is not easy – however, able is most common.
- Recap the rule: words that end in an **s** sound usually end in ible. Where the word root is not altered, usually add able.
- Which other adjective-forming suffixes do the children know? (ful, ic, etc.)

Homework Complete spellings using ible or able.

Oddbod queue
- Ask the class to write the first two letters.
- Chant the next three: '*e-u-e*'.
- Now chant the whole word: '*qu-e-u-e*'.
- Speedwrite *queue*, chanting it quietly, on dry-wipe boards.

Snip-snap Adding ly
- Write up the following words: *slowly, calmly, careful, hopeful, full, happy, crazy, shy.*
- Ask children to work out the rules: most words just add ly; if a word ends in ll just add y; words of two or more syllables that end in y – change the y to an i, then add ly, e.g. *happy – happily* but *shy – shyly.*
- Show Me: dictate ly words for children to write on dry-wipe boards.

> **NLS objectives for Unit 6**
>
> 6.1.W1   6.1.W2   6.1.W3

Part 2 | You need   OHT 6; dry-wipe boards or notebooks

Whole class
- Focus on the bottom half of the OHT and read the words, saying each one clearly.
- Ask the children to put the seven words into three categories on the basis of the pronunciation of the final ion, e.g.
  - **yun**: *onion, companion, billion*;
  - **un**: *legion, region*;
  - two syllables, **i-on**: *champion*.
- Find more words to add to each category.
  N.B. Depending upon dialect, *billion* might be pronounced **yun** or **i-on**.
    Other words may also be affected by dialect pronunciation.
- Write a sentence using some of the words, e.g. *My companion grew a billion onions*.

Review
- Look at the icons on the inside back cover of the Pupil's Book. Which sense do the children think could help them with spelling words ending in ion? (The spelling can be recalled by listening carefully to the sound of the ending.)
- Homework review.
- The most common ending is able. Words that end in an **s** sound usually end in ible. Where the base word is not altered, usually add able. Check the spellings in a dictionary if necessary.

Follow-up homework
- Find other ways of spelling the **yun** sound at the end of words.

Test dictation
OB   The queue to see the show was over a kilometre long.
A   I would not expect an elephant to be as gentle as that.
     The team tracked the lioness back to her den.
B   We brainstormed some ideas crazily before we started writing.
     There are a million things I want to do in the summer holidays.
C   In English this year we have learnt how lots of different words are spelt.

Snip-snap   ct or ed?
- Write up: *tracked, act, packed, pact, expect, picked, tact, deduct, fact, ducked, stocked*. Ask the children to read the words aloud. Listen to the end of each word and say which letters it sounds like.
- Show Me: children put the spellings into two groups: ones that end in ct and ones that do not. Why do some words end in ed?
- Ask the children to generalise a rule, e.g. the ed ending is used for the past tense of verbs.
- Catch-you-out: a few exceptions have other similar-sounding past tense endings, e.g. *crept, slept, learnt* (or *learned*), *spelt* (or *spelled*).

Snip-snap   Doobeedoo!
- Write up: *shoe, glue, true, blue, flew, chew, do, who, two, ewe, queue, knew, stew, view, zoo*. Ask the children to read the words aloud. Listen to the end of each word and say which letters it sounds like.
- Ask the children what they notice about the spelling of these words and what rules might explain this. Ask the children to generalise a rule, e.g. English words never in u and seldom in oo.
- Catch-you-out: emu is Portuguese, guru is Indian and caribou is North American.

21

7 Long words – unstressed vowels 2

<table>
<tr><td colspan="2">Objectives for Unit 7</td></tr>
<tr><td colspan="2">To use mnemonics; to spell unstressed vowels in polysyllabic words</td></tr>
</table>

Part 1

You need OHT 7; dry-wipe boards or notebooks; Pupil's Book pages 14–15; PCM 7

Whole class

- Together, sound out a word where all the vowels are easily heard, e.g. *carton*. Remind children that sometimes vowels are unpronounced or hard to hear because they are spoken quickly or quietly.
- Demonstrate by saying *separate* (adjective): we do not say 'sep-ah-rate' but 'sep-ruht'.
- Focus on the speech bubbles on the top half of the OHT, hiding the list of words. Explain that all the missing words have unstressed vowels. Read out the list and ask the children to choose which word fills each gap, spelling them on dry-wipe boards: *yesterday, nervous, today, prepared, interview, surprised, arrived*.
- Show Me: check the children's efforts and write the correct spellings on the OHT, underlining the unstressed vowels: yest<u>e</u>rday, nerv<u>ou</u>s, t<u>o</u>day, pr<u>e</u>pared, int<u>e</u>rview, s<u>u</u>rprised, <u>a</u>rrived.
- Discuss ways of remembering spellings of words with unstressed vowels, e.g.
  - over-pronounce the stressed vowels and focus on the others (*com-p<u>a</u>n-y*)
  - highlight words within words (*con-son-ant*);
  - make up a mnemonic (*I'm never* late *for* choco*late*).
- Introduce the oddbod: *definite* – see below.

Pupil activities

A: Distinguish between words with unstressed syllables and all stressed syllables. Find more compound words.
B: Work out ways to remember the spelling of words with unstressed vowels.
C: Work out mnemonics for words with unpronounced vowels.

Think about…: Ways of remembering which unstressed/unpronounced vowel occurs in a spelling (*history*).

Review

- Recap useful strategies for learning more difficult words and discuss others, e.g. segmenting, applying rules or knowledge of spelling patterns.
- Refer to the icons on the inside back cover of the Pupil's Book.

Homework

Work out ways to remember spellings of words containing unstressed vowels.

Oddbod   definite

- Explain that the root is from the French *fin*, meaning 'end'.
- This makes the beginning easy – *de* + *fin*.
- Relate it to the spelling of *infinite*.
- Chant the ending 'i-t-e' then speedwrite the word on dry-wipe boards.

Snip-snap   Bag of Tricks

- Pick a word with unstressed or unpronounced syllables, e.g. *Wednesday*, and model different ways of remembering the spelling: chanting the syllables, finding words within words (*wed, day*), making up a mnemonic (*wild elephants *d*on't *n*eed to *e*at *s*weet *d*oughnuts *a*ll *y*ear).
- Put children into groups and assign each another word, e.g. *dictionary, library, difference, literacy, separate, stationary*. Groups have to come up with a 'Bag of tricks' – at least three different strategies for remembering their word.

NLS objective for Unit 7

6.2.W4

Part 2 | **You need**   OHT 7; dry-wipe boards or notebooks

Whole class   ■ Focus on the speech bubbles on the bottom half of the OHT. Make sure that the children can distinguish between words with unstressed (but still pronounced) vowels and words with unpronounced vowels (e.g. the middle vowel in *interest*). Point out that with this word we write more syllables than we pronounce: we say 'intrest'; we write *interest*.

■ Show Me: As in Part 1, children write the missing words on dry-wipe boards: *interest, journalism, mystery, affairs, travel, different, capitals, temperature*. Ask them to underline the unstressed or unpronounced vowels. Check their efforts and write the correct spellings on the OHT.

■ Invent sentences using such words, and identify the unstressed or unpronounced vowels, e.g. *Vegetables are not fattening but chocolate is.* Note: the unstressed or unpronounced vowels may be affected by regional dialects.

Review   ■ Recap: some words contain unpronounced vowels (e.g. we say 'desprate' but we write *desperate*) which means we write more syllables than we pronounce. This can make spelling difficult.

■ Recap spelling strategies covered in Part 1 and ask children to share some of the strategies they used in the homework activity.

■ Homework review.

■ List any words that are still causing difficulty. Make sure that you use various strategies for remembering their spellings – the more the merrier!

Follow-up homework   ■ Ask the children to think of words that have unpronounced consonants.

Test dictation   OB   There is a definite benefit in eating lots of vegetables.

A   I had forgotten how chilly February can be.
The butterfly looked so graceful flying round the garden.

B   The champion football team won the match by eleven goals to one.
In mathematics we learnt how to do multiplication and division.

C   Although Pam's idea seemed ridiculous at first, her business soon became prosperous.

Snip-snap   al Words

■ Write up the words: *ways, ready, together, most, right, so, though*.

■ Ask children to write the words on their dry-wipe boards, adding al at the beginning of each.

■ What changes does this addition make to the meanings of the original words?

Snip-snap   Settle

■ Write up the word *settle* and children 'take a picture'.

■ Cover the word, then children speedwrite it on dry-wipe boards.

■ Children practise the word with eyes closed.

8 Words for argument

Objectives for Unit 8

To use independent spelling strategies; to spell words used in discussions and arguments

Part 1

You need   OHT 8; dry-wipe boards or notebooks; Pupil's Book pages 16–18; PCM 8

Whole class
- Focus on the top half of the OHT and read the words.
- The words, listed alphabetically, are all useful words for argument; for introducing discussion, putting across a point of view, putting the other side, or concluding.
- Revisit how we change words, e.g.
  - adding ing, ed, s;
  - change verb tense;
  - changing nouns to plural or singular;
  - adding a suffix to change the word class;
  - adding a prefix to change the meaning.
- Show Me: children suggest related words and write them on dry-wipe boards. Check spellings and add them to the OHT.
- Revisit words they find difficult and use relevant strategies for learning spellings.
- Can the children add to the list of root words?
- Introduce the oddbod: *argument* – see below.

Pupil activities
A: Find and list words related by meaning.
B: Find related words and use them in sentences.
C: Work out strategies for remembering spellings.

Extra challenge: Think of two ways to remember the spelling of *contradict*. Write two contradictory sentences.

Review
- Recap some ways in which we can change words. Ask children for an example of each way.
- Ask children for some examples of words which can't be changed in these ways. What kind of words are they? (e.g. connectives)

Homework   Find words based on the wh question words and use them in sentences.

Oddbod   argument

- This just has to be remembered – when you add ment onto *argue*, drop the e.
- Write up *argue* and children speedwrite *argument* on dry-wipe boards.

Snip-snap   Dominoes

- Write the word *domino* on the board.
- Teams take it in turns to add another interconnecting word.
- Each word added must use one letter of an existing word (like Scrabble).
- You score one point per letter used.

NLS objectives for Unit 8		
6.2.W1	6.2.W3	6.2.W8

Part 2 | You need   OHT 8; dry-wipe boards or notebooks

Whole class
- Revisit the top half of OHT 8 and read the words together.
- Remind the children that these words are useful for argument but the list is not exhaustive.
- Sort the words from the top half into the four categories in the bottom half. This activity is likely to stimulate much discussion as many words will fit into more than one category, depending upon context. Invite children to provide example sentences to illustrate a word's use in a particular category.
- Together, write a short passage to summarise a debate. Use as many of the words as possible, e.g. *We wish to debate the topic of football at playtime. Many people at school think that this would be a sensible option for playtimes because it keeps children healthy. Secondly, it keeps children occupied. On the other hand… Finally, having considered this argument from both sides…*

Review
- Consider the spelling strategies that would help with spelling these words. Refer to the inside back cover of the Pupil's Book and discuss which senses would be helpful for particular words.
- There are a number of words beginning with wh and the that are worth learning as a group – see Snip-snap wh and the words.

- Homework review.
- Children make an A4 class poster showing all the wh words they found.

Follow-up homework
- Ask children to make a note in their spelling logs of any useful words for writing arguments that they are unsure how to spell.

Test dictation
- OB Whenever Pat sees her enemy, they have a big argument.
- A Mr Black suddenly got into a terrible rage.
  I did not believe Jill's claim that she had met the famous actor.
- B I tried to see things from my sister's viewpoint.
  We don't know whether or not to expect rain tomorrow.
- C Tina was not convinced that the enormous snake was harmless.

Snip-snap Believe It or Not
- Make up a mnemonic for the spelling of *believe* (e.g. *there's an eve in believe*).
- On dry-wipe boards, children write as many related words as they can think of (e.g. *disbelieve, unbelievable, believer, belief*). Talk about how the word is changed when prefixes or suffixes are added or when the verb becomes a noun.

Snip-snap wh and the Words
- Quickfire spelling of question words beginning with wh, e.g. *when, where, who, why, what, which.*
- Quickfire spelling of words beginning with the, e.g. *then, there, their, these, they, them.*

9 Spelling rules and mnemonics

Objective for Unit 9

To apply spelling rules and create useful mnemonics

Part 1 | You need

OHT 9; dry-wipe boards or notebooks; Pupil's Book pages 18–19; PCM 9

Whole class

Mnemonics can be useful as an aid for spelling. There are different types – look at the top half of the OHT, which shows some examples. Together, try adding further examples to each one. Children often find the ones they make up the most memorable.

- Acrostics – making a phrase out of the letters of the spelling, e.g. *because* = *big elephants can always understand small elephants*.
- Pairs – some words are best learned in pairs or groups, especially if they rhyme and share a pattern, e.g. sing the refrain from the Beatles song, '*here, there and everywhere*'.
- Rhymes – short rhymes, or chanting words aloud to a rhythmic pattern, e.g. '*Mrs M, Mrs I, Mrs SSI, Mrs SSI, Mrs PPI*' = *Mississippi*.
- Words within words (even if they are nonsense words) – e.g. *There is a sti in nastiest* and *there is a sig in designed*.

Together, try writing some acrostics based around words that the children often mis-spell, or that they need in another subject area, e.g. *make every teacher ride elephants* = *metre*.

Introduce the oddbod: *embarrass* – see below.

Pupil activities

A: Use rhymes to remember spelling patterns and rules.
B: Use words within words to remember spellings.
C: Invent mnemonics.

Think about...: How to remember *ight*.

Review

Rules for spelling can be useful, but it is important to build up a bank of common exceptions as well as a range of other strategies for double-checking spelling. Mnemonics are a useful way of remembering tricky words: there are several basic types, e.g. rhymes, pairs, acrostics, and words within words.

Ask C group children to read out examples of the mnemonics they wrote in their independent work and ask the other children to guess which words they are for.

Homework

Invent mnemonics based on rhyming pairs of words.

Oddbod embarrass

- Introduce a mnemonic for *embarrassment*, e.g. Whenever Charlie stands and speaks, *I get two red ears and two scarlet cheeks*. Draw a face on the board with two red ears and scarlet cheeks.
- You can also remember it because embarrassment – is double trouble.

Snip-snap Mnemonic

- Mnemonic for embarrassment:
  Whenever Charlie stands and speaks,
  I get two red ears and two scarlet cheeks.
- Ask children to work out a mnemonic for other hard words, e.g. whisper, castle, plumber, occasion.

NLS objectives for Unit 9

6.2.W1　　6.2.W2　　6.2.W3　　6.2.W4

Part 2 | You need　OHT 9; dry-wipe boards or notebooks

Whole class
- Focus on the bottom half of the OHT and read the words.
- Encourage the children to try at least two mnemonics for each word.
- Evaluate the different types of mnemonics: what works for some children will almost certainly not be the best for others. Complete the chart to reflect the majority opinion.
- Write some sentences using the words, e.g. *They injured themselves while working on their individual design techniques.*

Review
- Recap the different types of mnemonics.
- Ask individual children to tell you a word they find difficult and, as a class, make up a mnemonic of one of these types.

- Homework review.
- Use these rhymes to help you recall the correct spelling – make sure that the word that you use as a rhyme is one that you can spell!

Follow-up homework
- Copy out key mnemonics that you will find useful. (Note that while some pupils find this method useful others cannot remember the mnemonic and therefore need to use other strategies.)

Test dictation
- OB If you misbehave in public you will only embarrass yourself.
- A　My bedroom curtains are made out of bright blue cloth.
  　When the weather is wet I like to travel by taxi.
- B　Having raspberry ice-cream for dinner is a real delight.
  　You must not forget to whisper when working in the library.
- C　The champion seemed so mighty and invincible that we didn't expect him to lose.

Snip-snap　Word Chant
- Who can spell *necessary*? Children write the word on dry-wipe boards.
- Introduce a well-known mnemonic for *necessary*: *It needs one collar and two socks.*
- 'Take a picture of the word', then chant 'one c, double s' and see a picture of one collar and two socks.
- Now spell *necessary*!

Snip-snap　Rainbow
- Ask children if they have been told mnemonics for other things they need to know, e.g. Richard of York gained battles in vain. (for the colours of the rainbow – red, orange yellow, green, blue, indigo, violet)
- Tell the children to chant this to themselves as they write the colours of the rainbow on their dry-wipe boards.

Objective for Unit 10

To consolidate on previous learning, applying spelling strategies and rules

Part 1 | **You need** — OHT 10; dry-wipe boards or notebooks; Pupil's Book pages 20–21; PCM 10

Whole class
- Focus on the top half of the OHT and read it together. Complete the chart with suggestions from the children. Ask them to write spellings on their dry-wipe boards.
- Invite the children to add to the chart.
- Write several sentences using some words that double up, e.g. *The frog hopped and then stopped*.
- Introduce the oddbod: *beginning* – see below.

Pupil activities
A: Investigate which consonants double.
B: Unscramble words that feature double consonants.
C: Investigate which consonants can double.

Extra challenge: Distinguish between *gorilla* and *guerrilla*.

Review
- Ask the children to sum up the rules for adding a suffix to one-syllable words with a short vowel before a single final consonant.
- Ask them to give you some examples of words which change in this way.

Homework
Investigate the spelling of verbs and adjectives that double their consonants.

Oddbod   beginning
- Break the word into parts: be + gin is easy (or beg + in).
- The end is common: ing.
- The only part to remember is doubling the n.

Snip-snap   Hissing Plurals
- Call out a word at a time from the following list: *guess, moth, torch, nose, toe, box, house, ice, miss, glass, bush, slice, wedge, branch, ranch*.
- Children stay sitting if the word just adds s in the plural, but stand up if it adds es – score a point if correct.
- Show Me: children earn an extra point by writing the word correctly on their dry-wipe boards.

NLS objectives for Unit 10			
6.2.W1	6.2.W2	6.2.W3	6.2.W4

Part 2 | You need   OHT 10; dry-wipe boards or notebooks

Whole class
- Focus on the bottom half of the OHT and read the list of words.
- Ask the children to identify the word class of each word.
- Add suffixes to each word, discussing whether the suffix changes the word class, e.g. *beauty* (noun) – *beauties* (noun) – beautiful (adj); *cry* (noun/verb) – *cries* (noun/verb) – *crying* (noun/verb) – *cried* (verb); *happy* (adj) – *happiness* (noun).
- Children try to spell each word + suffix on dry-wipe boards.
- Children investigate the rules, e.g.
  - What happens to consonant + y when you add a suffix? (it turns to i e.g. beauty – beautiful)
  - What happens to vowel + y when you add a suffix? (you just add it e.g. donkey – donkeys)
- Write correct spellings onto the OHT in the correct column.
- Write several sentences using some of the words, e.g. *I made many journeys on several donkeys.*

Review
- Ask the children to sum up the rules for making plurals of words ending in y.
- Ask them to give you examples of words which change in this way.

- Homework review.
- Summarise the rules for doubling consonants in verbs and adjectives.

Follow-up homework
- Make a note of useful rules and reminders.

Test dictation
- OB I read the beginning of the actor's biography, but didn't get to the end of it.
- A   I grabbed a biro and wrote my signature quickly.
       I hopped onto the bus and set off on my expedition.
- B   At the zoo I saw some monkeys with beautiful ginger fur.
       Evidence shows that most families argue sometimes.
- C   "My advice would be to take an umbrella with you," said Mum.

Snip-snap   Plurals
- Write up words ending in f, e.g. *thief, calf, self, scarf, wharf, turf, elf, loaf, half, wolf, sheaf, leaf.* Children write the plurals on dry-wipe boards.
- Ask children for a general rule – some words that end in f or fe change the f to v and add es (*thieves, knives*); others just add s (*chiefs*); words that end in ff always just add s (*cliffs*).

Snip-snap   Which One?
- Write up a pair of words, one spelt correctly and the other spelt with a common error (this could be taken straight from children's own common errors, e.g *intresting* for *interesting*).
- Children use a range of strategies to work out the correct spelling and write it on their board.
- Ask them to justify their response and explain strategies used, e.g. rules, patterns, root words, affixes, 'look', sound.

11 Word origins

Objectives for Unit 11

To investigate the origins of English words and to use word roots to aid spelling

| **Part 1** | **You need** | OHT 11; dry-wipe boards or notebooks; Pupil's Book pages 22–23; PCM 11 |

Whole class
- Explain that the roots of many English words come from other languages.
- Focus on the OHT and read through the Greek roots. The spellings may have changed slightly or been shortened since they were introduced.
- Ask children to match the English words to the Greek roots they come from and write these on their dry-wipe boards. They can add any others they can think of.
- Write definitions for some of the words, illuminating their origins, e.g. *Biography is writing about someone's life.*
- Introduce the oddbod: *technology* – see below.

Pupil activities
A: Match Greek and Latin roots to English words.
B: Find the meanings of words with Greek roots.
C: Find words that come from Greek roots.

Extra challenge: Find the origins of words that come from people's names. (*cardigan* – the woolly waistcoat introduced by the Earl of Cardigan in the Crimean War; *diesel* – from the engine invented by Rudolf Diesel; *wellingtons* – named after the boots worn by the 1st Duke of Wellington; *mesmerise* – from Dr Franz Mesmer, who used hypnotism)

Review
- Recap: the original meaning of words can be traced through their roots. These may come from many other languages, living or dead. This knowledge can be useful in understanding spelling.
- Ask children to share some of the results of their independent investigations.
- Prepare for homework by showing the class how the root of a word is indicated in a dictionary.

Homework
Collect more words based on Greek roots.

Oddbods technology
- What does ology mean? ('science' or 'study of') Discuss definitions of various ology words, e.g. *archaeology, astrology, criminology, ecology, ornithology, psychology, zoology.*
- Tech can be remembered by saying it as it is written, pronouncing the ch as in cheese.

Snip-snap French Words
- Say a word with French origins and ask the children to write it on their dry-wipe boards.
- Discuss meanings and origins of words as well as strategies needed for spelling harder words.
- Use *café, restaurant, mousse* ('moss'), *rampant* (*ramper* – 'to clamber'), *chivalry* (*cheval* – 'horse'), *champagne* (from the area), *environment* (*environ* – 'around').

NLS objectives for Unit 11

6.2.W2   6.2.W3   6.2.W4   6.2.W5

Part 2 | You need   OHT 11; dry-wipe boards or notebooks; spelling logs

Whole class
- Focus on the bottom half of the OHT and read through the Latin roots.
- Ask children to think of any English words they know that are based on each Latin root, e.g. *reaction, aqualung, audible, capital, benefactor, manual, maritime, optimistic, pedestrian, survive.*
- Write definitions for some of the words children suggest, illuminating their origins, e.g. *manufacture means 'to make something by hand'*.

Review
- Recap: words in our language come from languages around the world and have changed over time. Many words have their origins in Greek and Latin. Reinforce the idea that knowing their roots can help spelling.

- Homework review.
- Make a note of the most common Greek or Latin roots and their meanings. Some dictionaries provide information on roots. Use this when spelling.

Follow-up homework
- Note common Greek and Latin roots and use these to help with spelling.

Test dictation

OB My new computer has all the latest hardware technology.
A   My concern was that the curry would be too hot to eat.
    It was so cold yesterday that I put on a cardigan over my nightie.
B   I think that algebra is the most difficult part of mathematics.
    The cyclone dragged the little house into the sea.
C   Jim concluded that he liked raspberry mousse better than chocolate.

Snip-snap   Indian Words
- Say a word with Indian origins and ask children to write it on their dry-wipe boards.
- Discuss meaning and origins of words as well as strategies needed for harder words.
- Use *bungalow, jodhpurs, pyjamas, thug, shampoo, khaki, curry, veranda, juggernaut.*

Snip-snap   Arabic Words
- Say the word *algebra* and ask children to write it on their dry-wipe boards.
- Discuss the meaning and origin of the word (from Arabic *al-jebr* meaning 'combination') and go on to discuss other words of Arabic origin, e.g. *sugar* (from *sukkar*), *admiral* (from *amir-al-bahr* – 'lord of the sea'), *alcohol* (from *al-koh'l* – 'powder for staining the eyelids'), *monsoon* (*mausim* – 'a time or season').

12 Revisiting suffixes and prefixes

Objectives for Unit 12

To investigate the use of suffixes and prefixes; to develop the ability to proofread

| **Part 1** | **You need** | OHT 12; dry-wipe boards or notebooks; Pupil's Book pages 24–25; PCM 12 |

Whole class

- Focus on the top half of the OHT and read the sentences.
- Ask: what do the underlined words mean? What are the word roots and what do the prefixes mean? (auto – 'self', un – 'not', re – 'again')
- Children suggest and spell on dry-wipe boards other words that use these prefixes, e.g. *automatic, unhappy, return*. List them on the OHT.
- Write up any other prefixes that the children know, e.g. anti, pre, in, im, super, sub, etc.
- Write several sentences using common prefixes, e.g. *I wish to replace the television, as it was a mistake.*
- Introduce the oddbod: *skilful* – see below.

Pupil activities

A: Use prefixes to create opposites.
B: Investigate 'size' prefixes (e.g. hyper, micro).
C: Investigate suffixes by making words.

Extra challenge: Investigate the suffix ology.

Review

- There are prefixes that are not words in their own right (e.g. im, in, re) and there are prefixes that are (e.g. super, photo). The latter are used to make compound words. Can the children suggest some?
- This knowledge can help you to spell more effectively and to be more adventurous with your choice of words. Why use *star* when *megastar* says so much more? Does it have a different meaning?

Homework

Choose the correct spelling of words in a passage. Identify any prefixes and suffixes.

Oddbod *skilful*

- Revisit the rule – when full is used as a suffix, one l is dropped, e.g. *useful, careful, handful*.
- Write up the following word sums: *will + full = wilful, full + fill = fulfil*.
- Work out the rule and apply it to: *skill + full*.

Snip-snap Common Errors

- Write up *surprise/suprise*. Ask children to tell you which one looks right.
- Ask children why they think this mistake was made (because we don't hear the r when the word is spoken). How can you remember the correct spelling?
- Repeat with the following word pairs: *targit/target, complane/complain, serius/serious, unusal/unusual, loudly/loudley*, or use others from the children's own writing.

NLS objectives for Unit 12

6.2.W1   6.2.W2   6.2.W3   6.2.W4   6.2.W5

Part 2 | You need   OHT 12; dry-wipe boards or notebooks

Whole class
- Read through the sentences on the bottom half of the OHT.
- Ask: what might the suffixes in the words underlined mean? (less means 'without' or 'having no'; er means 'person or thing that does something' (added to verbs) or 'more' (added to adjectives); ness can be added to an adjective to make a noun, meaning the quality indicated by the adjective; ship can be added to a noun to show the status of the person; like can be added to nouns to make an adjective that means 'having that characteristic')
- List any other suffixes that the children know, e.g. ology, ist, let, wise, ish, dom, hood, ism, ation, ic.
- Write some sentences using common suffixes, e.g. *The teacher is an organiser, entertainer, trainer, juggler, soother and sweetener.*

Review
- Recap: suffixes are attached to word roots to make different meanings and may change the word class. Knowledge of suffixes can help with spellings but also helps you to choose more interesting words.
- As a class, brainstorm some interesting words with suffixes which could help improve children's writing.

- Homework review.
- When spelling, use knowledge of prefixes and suffixes to help. Sometimes concentrating on a word and trying it out a few times can help you get the correct spelling. Or use a dictionary or IT spell-check. Always proofread your work.

Follow-up homework
- List useful prefixes and suffixes to assist with spelling. Get into the habit of rapid double-checking of spellings. Get to know the words that you find tricky. Keep a list of correct spellings for these words.

Test dictation
- OB You have to be both skilful and calm to be an optician.
- A   I had forgotten that my right trainer had a hole in it.
       Please could you explain to me how to send an e-mail?
- B   My brother isn't unattractive, but he can be very antisocial.
       Lisa was graceful, gentle and famous for her kindness.
- C   You can buy millions of different things in our local hypermarket.

Snip-snap   Mis-spellings
- Write up sentences that have some incorrectly spelt words, e.g. *My unckle fell asleap in the cinama and snorred.*
- Show Me: children write the correct spellings on their dry-wipe boards.
- Discuss why mistakes were made and strategies for checking.
- Use common errors from children's own writing.

Snip-snap   Roots
- Write up a word root. Ask the children to say aloud a word based on it, e.g. aero – *aeroplane.*
- Show Me: write up more word roots and ask children to write related words on dry-wipe boards. Try: text, script, sign, port, confer, shine, quake.

13 Confusables

Objective for Unit 13

To investigate words that often get muddled because they look or sound similar

Part 1 | You need

OHT 13; dry-wipe boards or notebooks; Pupil's Book pages 26–27; PCM 13

Whole class

- Focus on the top half of the OHT. Read all the words together. Which words sound the same?
- Find and discuss the meanings of the words as you match the pairs.
- Examine the spellings. Talk about alternative ways of spelling sounds. Which are the more common ways? e.g. **ed** ending and **wh** beginning.
- Show Me: give a sentence in which one of the words from an often-confused pair is included. Children write the correct spelling on dry-wipe boards, then check them. Repeat as many times as necessary and with different words from the list.
- Encourage the children to make up a sentence for a partner to try, jotting down their sentences on dry-wipe boards, spelling the words correctly.
- Write several sentences using pairs of confusable words, e.g. *The principal has strong principles. You two can help to tidy, too.*
- Introduce the oddbods: *advice, advise* – see below.

Pupil activities

A: Write sentences using pairs of common homophones.
B: Write sentences using two words that look similar.
C: Identify triple homophones and identify confusables in own work.

Extra challenge: Find homophone pairs.

Review

- To distinguish between 'confusables' (words that look or sound similar) pay attention to the meaning and context.
- Try some of the Snip-snap homophone riddles (see below).

Homework

Choose *of, off* or *have* to complete sentences.

Oddbods   *advise, advice*

- The simplest way to recall which is which is to ensure that the words are pronounced clearly: *I* ad**vise** *you* (**ise** as in *eyes*) and *my* ad**vice** (**ice** as in *ice*).
- The noun is *advice* – and has a **c** in it (*ice* and *vice* are both nouns).
- The verb is *advise* – and has an **s** in it.

Snip-snap   Homophone Riddles

- Ask children to find and spell the homophone pairs to answer these riddles:
  What opens locks and is always found beside water?
  What starts a letter and is also an animal?
  What is a colour and what the wind does?
  What stands in shining armour and is black?
- Encourage the children to make up more examples.

NLS objectives for Unit 13	
6.3.W3	6.3.W4

Part 2 | **You need**   OHT 13; dry-wipe boards or notebooks

Whole class
- Focus on the bottom half of the OHT and read the words in each column.
- Discuss why confusion occurs.
- Discuss strategies for remembering which spelling goes with which meaning, taking account of apostrophes, tense, mnemonics, etc.
- Draw attention to the problems caused by *could've/should've*, which is an abbreviation of *could/should have* but is sometimes written incorrectly as *could/should of*.
- Write sentences that demonstrate understanding, using the correct spelling, e.g. *You're holding your future in your hands. They should've known better than to go alone.*

Review
- Recap: children can distinguish between confusables by meaning and context.
- Discuss spelling strategies which can be used to double-check words.
- Homework review.
- Collect examples of tricky words gleaned from homework. How many have unstressed or 'lost' (elided) vowels? Start a class collection or add to the OHT.

Follow-up homework
- Make a list of any words that are still causing confusion, especially those with contractions.

Test dictation
- OB I would advise you not to swim too far away from the shore.
- A   Being a champion at sport is a real feat.
       Elves have very small feet.
- B   If you pull that cord, the train will stop suddenly.
       Jane played a chord on the piano.
- C   "You'll just have to accept that I snore at night," said Dad.

Snip-snap   Homophones
- Write up pairs of words, e.g. *meter/metre*.
- Children write, on their dry-wipe boards, silly sentences in which both words are used and their different meanings demonstrated, e.g. *My meter can record how many metres you can fly.*
- Try: *peer/pier, read/reed, rain/reign, heel/heal, wait/weight, ring/wring, pain/pane, maid/made, cord/chord.*

Snip-snap   Topsy-turvy
- Take three-, four- or five-letter words and change their letters round to make them into other words, e.g. *slap* becomes *pals*.
- Try: *dog, bat, rat, not, pot, pit, tap, stab, pore, lips, shop, stun, flog, times, slime.*
- Children can suggest more words for a partner to change.

Spelling rules and strategies 2

Objective for Unit 14

To revise the use of spelling rules and strategies

Part 1 | **You need** | OHT 14; dry-wipe boards or notebooks; Pupil's Book pages 28–29; PCM 14

Whole class
- Focus on the top half of the OHT 14 and read the extract from *A Midsummer's Night Dream*. Discuss its meaning.
- Show me: ask the children to take each word, segment it and underline the parts that make any of the following sounds: **ai**, **ee**, **ie**, **oa**, **oo**. Then they can list the different spellings for each sound:
  ai: *apricots* (a), *grapes* (a-e)
  ee: *be, courteous* (e), *feed, green, bees* (ee), *steal* (ea), *honey* (ey)
  ie: *kind* (i), *eyes* (eye)
  oa: (no words)
  oo: *dewberries* (ew)
- Discuss any patterns and ambiguities (e.g. *courteous*).
- Compose some sentences using other words with these sounds, e.g. *Soon the kangaroo will fly in a blue balloon.*
- Introduce the oddbod: *although* – see below.

Pupil activities
A: Find words in a poem with the 'long' **ai** phoneme and investigate spelling patterns.
B: Sort words with 'long' **ee** and 'long' **oo** phonemes. Investigate spelling patterns.
C: Sort words with 'long' **ie** and 'long' **oa** phonemes. Investigate spelling patterns.

Extra challenge: Investigate the spelling of words that end with an **ai** sound.

Review
- When spelling, various strategies can help: segmenting words, listening to the vowel sounds and thinking about the most likely spelling.
- Children practise segmenting some of the polysyllabic words from their independent activities (e.g. *verify, supply, beautiful, machine, shoulder, apply, swallow*).

Homework
Sort words by their 'long' vowel sound.

Oddbod   although
- Revisit the rule for using all as a prefix by listing *always, almost, already, altogether.*
- What is the rule? (Like adding full as a suffix, drop one l).
- Chant 'o-u-g-h' to help memorise spelling.
- List other ough words, e.g. *bough, cough, dough, plough, rough, tough.* Discuss differences in pronunciation.
- 'Take a picture' of the word and then speedwrite on dry-wipe boards to see who can write *although* the greatest number of times in 30 seconds.

Snip-snap   Reveal
- Take a word, e.g. *butterfly* and write up the first letter: b.
- Children guess the next letter, writing it on dry-wipe boards.
- Then write up the second letter, making bu. Children adjust their ideas about the word.
- Obviously the choices narrow the more letters you write up. Challenge children to guess and spell aloud the word you are thinking of. To gain a point the word must be guessed and spelled correctly. Otherwise, continue until the final letter.

NLS objectives for Unit 14		
6.3.W2	6.3.W3	6.3.W4

Part 2 | **You need**   OHT 14; dry-wipe boards or notebooks

Whole class
- First reread the extract on the top part of the OHT.
- Then focus on the bottom half of the OHT and read the beginning of the rewritten extract. What do the children notice about the rewritten beginning?
- Show Me: ask the children to suggest adjectives and nouns with 'long' vowel phonemes to fill in the gaps and to change the original meaning e.g.

> *Feed him with <u>earwigs</u> and <u>centipedes</u>,*
> *With <u>blue</u> <u>spiders</u>, <u>grey</u> <u>mice</u> and <u>butterfly</u> <u>feelers</u>;*
> *The <u>eyes</u> steal from the <u>slimy</u> <u>snakes</u>,*

- They write their attempt on dry-wipe boards first. Then discuss spelling choices together.

Review
- Knowing the options for spelling 'long' vowel phonemes can help you to spell more confidently and accurately.
- Remind the children of other vowel phonemes (e.g. **or**, **er**, **oy**, **ar**). Can they suggest common spelling patterns for each of these?
- Homework review.
- Segmentation can help identify 'long' vowel sounds. Think carefully about the most likely spelling – watch the endings, e.g. **ay**, **ee** or **ea**.

Follow-up homework
- Find a passage from a reading book or the children's own writing and change its meaning by changing adjectives and nouns that use 'long' vowel phonemes.

Test dictation
OB   Although Dad has read a manual, he still doesn't understand the Internet.
A   Tom looked at the balloon with childlike joy.
     The brake on my bicycle does not work when it is wet.
B   We watched the replay of the Queen's Christmas speech.
     I felt a pain when I dropped a big stone on my foot.
C   You should verify my claim before you contradict it.

Snip-snap   Impossible Endings
- Say a word that sounds as if it might end in u, i, j or v, e.g. *true, shoe, flew, do, try, cry, supply, apply, wedge, ledge, bridge, salve, nerve, grave, cove, dove.*
- Children spell the word on dry-wipe boards.
- You or their partner check spellings. Summarise by noting that generally, English words do not end in u, i, j or v.

Snip-snap   Quickfire Spelling
- On dry-wipe boards, ask children to write words that start with al and words that end with ful. Try: *always, altogether, although, also, always, almost, handful, cupful, forgetful, skilful, wishful, hopeful, painful.*
- Summarise by noting that they begin with al, not all and end with ful, not full.

Objectives for Unit 15

To identify spellings used to represent dialects; to use mnemonics as an aid to spelling

Part 1 | You need

OHT 15; dry-wipe boards or notebooks; Pupil's Book pages 30–31; PCM 15

Whole class

- As an introduction, talk about the different ways that people speak. Focus on the top half of the OHT 15 and explain that this poem has been written in dialect. This unit requires a degree of sensitivity if you are teaching in an area where this is the accent used. You read the poem first (in a caricature of an East London accent), and then ask the children to read it (with feeling).

- Explain that this poem was written with spellings of words that represent a regional dialect. Discuss why it has been deliberately written to reflect the way the words are spoken in this accent.

- Taking one line at a time, ask the children to rewrite the words with conventional spellings. Encourage different spelling strategies. Children write the correct spellings on dry-wipe boards.

- Together, write some more lines of the poem in dialect, e.g.:
  Your biby 'as fell dahn the plug 'ole,
  'E's in a better place.
  'E never liked being barfed with soap,
  'Specially on his face!

- Then rewrite the dialect words with conventional spellings.
- Introduce the oddbod: *questionnaire* – see below.

Pupil activities

A: Correct the spellings in a passage.
B: Invent mnemonics.
C: Identify dialect spellings in the second verse of *Biby's Epitaph* and change to conventional spellings.

Think about…: The silent w in *two*.

Review

- Discuss when you might want to use unconventional spellings in your work, e.g. to build on characterisation. It requires quite a sophisticated knowledge of spelling rules to get it right!
- What strategies might you use to write such a piece?

Homework

Choose the correct spelling of words in a passage.

Oddbod *questionnaire*

- Build up question – q + u + est (*quest* rhymes with *west*) + tion ending.
- Add on naire (there is *air* in naire).
- Chant 'n-a-i-r-e'. Write the whole word on the board, chant the spelling, 'take a picture', then rub it out.
- Speedwrite the word to help memorise, then check.

Snip-snap Which One?

- Write up pairs or groups of correctly and incorrectly spelt words. Children write down the correct spelling on dry-wipe boards and show.
- Try using common errors in children's own writing as well as words needed in different curriculum areas, e.g.: *rime/ryhme/rhyme, wagan/wagon, guage/gauge, terribul/terrible/terribel, forety/fourty/forty, inclose/enclose, woolen/woollen.*

NLS objectives for Unit 15

6.3.W1   6.3.W3   6.3.W4

Part 2 | You need   OHT 15; dry-wipe boards or notebooks

Whole class

- Focus on the bottom half of the OHT and revisit the basic types of mnemonic, e.g. rhymes, pairs, words within words, and acrostics.
- The children categorise the examples shown.
- Show Me: children write more examples for each of the categories on dry-wipe boards.
- Focus on the spellings of *advice/advise* and *practice/practise*. If in doubt, knowing the word class can help – c comes before s in the alphabet and n (noun) comes before v (verb).
- Compose some sentences using some of the words on the OHT or ones for which the class have invented mnemonics, e.g. *I advise you to take my advice. Can I practise my cooking skills by getting some practice at cooking for you?*

Review

- Mnemonics can be useful when there is no other easy way to learn a spelling.
- Children should also remember to use all of their senses to help remember spellings: refer to the icons on the inside back cover of the Pupil's Book.

- Homework review.
- In pairs, children compare spellings. If there are any disagreements they should check in a dictionary.

Follow-up homework

- Ask the children to write out their favourite mnemonic.

Test dictation

OB You don't have to fill in the questionnaire – it's voluntary.

A   My aunt will be forty on her next birthday.
     I begged Mum to get me a kangaroo for Christmas.

B   If you want to take up exercise, it helps to have a trainer.
     Unfortunately, the expedition to the moon ended in disaster.

C   Zoology, psychology and astronomy are certainly sciences.

Snip-snap   Confusables

- Write up sentences that contain a few common 'confusables', e.g. *I will except a peace of cake. I right on a large bored. The dog's tale is two lose.*
- Children work in pairs to write the correct spellings on dry-wipe boards.

Snip-snap   Right or Wrong?

- Write up words where mistakes are often made, spelling some correctly and some incorrectly. Children put thumbs up or down, depending on whether they think the word is correctly spelt.
- Try: *familiar, handful, disease, exercise, piece, happily, shyly, timely, quickest, saddest, daring, begged, benefit, compelling.*

Objectives for Unit 16

To spell words using known spellings of other words with similar patterns; spelling words with silent letters

---

Part 1

You need OHT 16; dry-wipe boards or notebooks; Pupil's Book pages 32–33; PCM 16

Whole class

- Focus on the top half of the OHT and discuss the words in the first column. What makes them similar? (They all rhyme – depending on regional accents; rhyme can be a help as a spelling strategy but it has its limitations.) Discuss variations in spelling.
- Ask the children what makes the words in the second column similar. (They all share the same spelling pattern but each is pronounced differently.) Point out that this mismatch between spelling pattern and sound creates problems. Ask children to think of some words with the same spelling pattern that rhyme with *tough* (e.g. *rough, enough*). Explain that the other words in the column need memorising!
- The third list demonstrates that rhyme can be helpful in some instances. Show Me: children write further rhyming words that share the same pattern on their dry-wipe boards. There are at least 13 more. (*quack, rack, sack, shack, slack, smack, snack, stack, tack, thwack, track, whack, wrack*)
- Write a few silly sentences using the words from the OHT, e.g. *Although I got caught, the court thought that I was tough enough to walk through fire without a single cough!*
- Introduce the oddbod: *diamond* – see below.

Pupil activities

A: Make lists of words related by rhyme and spelling pattern.
B: Make lists of words related by spelling pattern and by meaning.
C: Investigate gh spelling patterns.

Think about...: 'Tricky' words that just have to be learnt.

Review

- Rhyme can help with some words – and it gets you thinking about possibilities. Learning by pattern is also useful; again it helps you know what a spelling might be. Using meaning can also help to make links.
- Ask children to suggest words they find hard to spell, and, as a class, make suggestions for rhymes, patterns and meanings to help them remember.

Homework Investigate the phoneme **k**.

Oddbod   *diamond*

- Learn the word by saying it as it is spelt: '*di-a-mond*'.
- List other dia words, e.g. *diameter, diary, diagnose, diagram*.
- Chant the word in its three parts, 'take a picture', then speedwrite and check.

Snip-snap   Beat the Clock

- You provide a word ending and children list, in 30 seconds, rhyming words that share the same spelling pattern. There are 37 dependable rimes (you might want to go steady with **ock, uck**, etc).
- Try: **ack, ail, ain, ake, ale, ame, an, ank, ap, ash, at, ate, aw, ay, eat, ell, est, ice, ick, ide, ight, ill, in, ine, ing, ink, ip, it, ock, oke, op, ore, ot, uck, ug, ump, unk.**

NLS objectives for Unit 16

6.3.W1   6.3.W4

Part 2 | **You need**   OHT 16; dry-wipe boards or notebooks

Whole class
- Focus on the bottom half of the OHT and read all the words.
- Ask the children what all the words have in common. (silent letters)
- Ask the children what the linked words in the example have in common. (the gn pattern)
- Get Up and Go: invite the children to find triplets where three words have matching silent letter patterns. Link them on the OHT with a line, as shown in the first example.
- Challenge the children to find an additional word for each triplet.
- Challenge the children to make a sentence using all three words e.g. to describe the illustration: *the ghastly ghost ate a gherkin.*
- Are these words that you just have to know, or can the children suggest helpful ways to remember the spellings?

Review
- Ask the children to remind you which letters are sometimes silent.
- Pronouncing all of the letters can help spell words like this.
- It can also be helpful to learn words with silent letters in groups.

- Homework review.
- Point out that the phoneme **k** has more ways of being spelt than any other sound in English. There are many different spelling possibilities which can occur at the beginning, middle and ends of words.
- The phoneme **ks** can be represented by cks, cs, x, xc, cc. At the beginning of words in English, ks is pronounced as 'z' (*xylophone*).

Follow-up homework
- Use different tactics for finding and learning spellings. Good spellers use lots of strategies – and pay attention to words.

Test dictation
OB My sister is delighted with her new diamond ring.
A   A quarter of a chocolate cake is just about digestible.
    There are many more hypermarkets on the continent than here.
B   The general was compelling the corporal to do more exercises.
    My sister was taught to practise her cello every day.
C   I know it's not logical, but I'm sure there is a ghost in our cellar.

Snip-snap   Picture It 👁 👄 ✏ 💭
- Write up a word, e.g. *astronomy*. Children 'take a picture', look carefully, repeat the word as written, exaggerating each sound.
- Cover the word and children speedwrite it on dry-wipe boards, read back to check, then show.
- Try: *corporal, January, mathematics, parallel, jewellery, alcohol, consonant, locomotive, signature, grammar.*

Snip-snap   gh Wipe-off 👁 💭 🧠
- Write up a list of around 10 words with gh, e.g. *bough, though, sleigh, weigh, through, sleight, night, fright, weight, caught, fraught, bought, ought, sought, cough, rough.*
- Give children a couple of minutes to study the words.
- Swoop suddenly on one word and wipe it off.
- Children write that word on dry-wipe boards, then check the spelling.

Part 1 | **You need** OHT 17; dry-wipe boards or notebooks; dictionaries; Pupil's Book pages 34–35; PCM 17

Whole class
- Focus on the top half of the OHT and ask the children if they know any jokes!
- Read the jokes one by one and discuss the spelling points associated with each. Explain puns and justify spelling changes.
  - *Where do dim witches go? Spelling classes!*
    Word association of *witch* and *spell*.
  - *What is the plural of mouse? Mice! What is the plural of house? Hice! What is the plural of baby? Twins!*
    Using a rule and applying it incorrectly followed by a catch-you-out.
  - *Give me a sentence with the word politics in it. Our parrot swallowed the alarm clock and now poli-tics!*
    A play on the words *politics* and *Polly* (a nickname for a parrot) and *ticks*.
  - *Please Miss, I've swallowed my pencil sharpener. You must be choking! No Miss, I'm perfectly serious!*
    A play on the words *choking* and *joking*.
  - *What do you get if you look at a vampire teacher through a telescope? A horror-scope!*
    A play on the words *horror* and *horoscope* – something different altogether.
  - *Where do skinny teachers train? At puny-versity!*
    A play on *puny* and *university*. This last joke can be extended ad infinitum, e.g. alien teachers (*moony-versity*), music teachers (*tuney-versity*).
- Introduce the oddbod: *consequence* – see below.

Pupil activities
A: Solve anagrams.
B: Solve anagrams and use the answers in sentences.
C: Solve and invent anagrams.

Extra challenge: Brainstorm other forms of language play, finding examples.

Review
- Ask children to share their favourite word-based jokes, riddles and puns.

Homework
Do a con crossword. Answers: *conkers, conceal, continue, confusion, connection, conversation*.

Oddbod consequence
- Look carefully at the word and break it up.
  - con is as it sounds.
  - se has only one e.
  - q must be followed by u.
  - quen rhymes with *men*.
  - The ending ce is the same as in *sequence*.
  - Learn as a double: *sequences have consequences*.

Snip-snap Collective Nouns
- Invent topsy-turvy collective nouns.
- An ordinary one might be: *a coldness of snow*.
- Now make the first part into an opposite: *a warmth of snow*.
- Write up a list of possible subjects, e.g. *stars, leaves, trees, rain, wasps, birds, trout, eggs, teachers, pencils, chocolate bars*.
- Children compose their ideas on dry-wipe boards, aiming for topsy-turvy collective nouns, e.g. *a heavyweight of clouds*.

NLS objectives for Unit 17

6.3.W6   6.3.W7

Part 2 | You need   OHT 17; dry-wipe boards or notebooks

Whole class
- Focus on the bottom half of the OHT and read through the spoonerisms together. Spoonerisms are named after the Rev W.A. Spooner from Oxford, who kept getting his words muddled. The technical name for the transposition of letters or sounds in a word is *metathesis*.
- Demonstrate how to work out the real meanings of the sentences.
- Show Me: Look at the pairs of words and invite the children to spoonerise them, e.g. *lacked punch*, *better locks*, *bounder's rat*, writing their responses on dry-wipe boards.
- Encourage the children to invent their own spoonerisms. They don't necessarily have to make sense!
- Children write their suggestions on their dry-wipe boards
- Create class spoonerisms together.

Review
- Recap: point out that playing with crosswords, riddles and other word games can improve spelling.
- Homework review.
- Children make a class collection of jokes.

Follow-up homework
- Play this game the next time that you are on a journey. Invent sentences based on the number plates that you see, e.g. Y612 EGL could be Elephants Grow Lettuces.

Test dictation
OB I had a hole in my pocket and, as a consequence, lost all my money.
A   I like to read my anthology of stories before I go to bed.
    Her daughter has some beautiful antique jewellery.
B   That unattractive caterpillar will soon transform into a butterfly.
    The crazy farmer decided to wrestle to win the cattle.
C   The convict appeared before the supreme court.

Snip-snap Alliteration
- Take one word as a starting point. This could be an animal, e.g. *dog*.
- Write it up and build words around it to create a tongue twister, e.g. *The dull, dirty, devious dog dug a deep ditch directly.*
- Brainstorm a list of other animals.
- Children rapidly write sentences using as much alliteration as possible.

Snip-snap Anagrams
- Write up a list of three-, four- and five-letter words, e.g. *ban, nib, dam, bad, bat, boy, but, bud, sag, saw, mad, map, may, mug, slip, stew, stop, slap, slime, strap, brag, sword, team.*
- Juggle with the spelling of a few to show how another word can be constructed by moving letters around, e.g. *ant* becomes *tan*, *nib* becomes *bin*, *sword* becomes *words*.
- Children do the same on dry-wipe boards within a time limit.

Objective for Unit 18

To invent new words by manipulating letters, using knowledge of spelling rules and morphology

---

| **Part 1** | **You need** | OHT 18; dry-wipe boards or notebooks; Pupil's Book pages 36–37; PCM 18 |

Whole class
- Focus on the top half of the OHT. Point out how the title *Poerse* is a mixture of the two words poetry and *verse*. Explain that words made by combining other words are called 'portmanteau' words.
- Read the poem. Ask the children to study the invented words and the pairs of words that they were made from.
- Get Up and Go: ask volunteers to underline the parts that were used to create new words. Which invented words do the children think are the most successful and actually sound like their meaning?
- Compose further examples. Write down a sentence using two verbs, e.g. *I saw a dog barking and growling at a postman*. Then blend the two verbs into one, e.g. *I saw a dog barling at a postman*.
- Introduce the oddbod: *outrageous* – see below.

Pupil activities
A: Invent names for animals from nouns and adjectives.
B: Invent new adverbs by combining verbs and adverbs.
C: Invent new words from prefixes, suffixes and word roots.

Extra challenge: Suggest meanings for some words from 'Jabberwocky'.

Review
- Ask children to share some of the words they made in their independent activities.
- Remind children that when creating new words, they have to keep thinking about letter patterns, sounds and meaning. This helps with spelling and can be fun!

Homework
Find words made from endings and beginnings of other words in sentences. Answers: *mew, rein, rear, ear, hath, vet, gin, none, new, rend, din, then, hen, two*; *rear, requite, tea, team, am, stop, top, topic, sop, sea, seat, onto, tot, heap, these*; *era, rat, rate, tea, ago, forest, rest, evil, get, toe, toes, pet, let, rerun, ground.*

Oddbod outrageous
- Break the word into three parts and say clearly 'out-rage-ous' to make spelling easy.
- *out* and *rage* are both easy: *outrage*.
- The suffix ous means 'full of', i.e. 'full of outrage'.
- Look at these words, comparing the first and last two.
  - danger + ous = dangerous
  - joy + ous = joyous
  - nerve + ous = nervous
  - adventure + ous = adventurous
- Draw up a rule: ous is added straight onto a word ending in a consonant. Where a silent e is the final letter, it is dropped.
- However, in outrage if the final e was dropped it would make the g a hard sound, 'out-rag', so the e has to be kept, making *outrage + ous*.

Snip-snap Rhyme
- Everyone starts with three points.
- One child says a word and the next person has to come up with a rhyme, passing it on until someone is stumped. This person loses a point – but starts the next round.
- The rhymes must share the same end spelling.
- Extra points can be gained by challenging someone, if a child thinks that the suggested rhyme is spelt differently. Gain or lose a point according to whether the challenge is correct.

NLS objectives for Unit 18

6.3.W5   6.3.W6   6.3.W7

Part 2 | **You need**   OHT 18; dry-wipe boards or notebooks; a reading book per child

Whole class   ■ Focus on the bottom half of the OHT and look at the example together. Explain that the word inside the brackets is a complete word itself, but it also ends the first word and begins the second, e.g. *razor* and *ornate* are joined by *or*.

■ Show Me: children work in pairs to find the words and write their ideas on dry-wipe boards. Allow about 30 seconds per word, and then check the answers: *domi(no)thing*; *sh(out)side*; *mis(take)away*; *comm(on)wards*; *spa(row)ingboat*; *for(ward)robe*; *cup(board)room*.

■ Together, put each pair of words into a sentence, e.g. *My dad has an ornate razor. Nothing could stop me playing dominoes.*

Review   ■ Remind children that playing with words can help them develop a love of words and an understanding of patterns, parts and meanings.

■ Homework review.

■ Ask children to check with a partner for any words they might have missed in their work on the PCM.

Follow-up homework   ■ Children play word games like *Scrabble* at wet playtimes to tune up spelling muscles.

Test dictation   OB My favourite aunt could not resist buying the outrageous hat.

A   People don't eat fattening food if they want to stay slender.
Science and technology are always moving forward.

B   My uncle swims well, loves sport and is very athletic.
Bob will stubbornly argue that his viewpoint is the right one.

C   If you get drenched in a submarine, it's a disaster.

Snip-snap   Quickfire ⊙ ✍ 💬

■ Write up a long word and children write down all the words that can be made from the letters, working on dry-wipe boards, e.g. *surprising – sir, sip, sin, sing, sips, sins, sips, sirs, sup, sups, pus, puss, pun, puns, pig, pigs, etc.*

■ Try: *categorisation, revolutionaries, metamorphose, antediluvian.*

Snip-snap   Adverbs 💬 ⊙ ⊖ 🎵 ✍

■ One child leaves the room. Everyone else decides on an adverb of manner, e.g. *slowly.*

■ The child returns and tries to find out what the adverb is by asking classmates to perform tasks, e.g. 'sing a song.' The chosen classmate has do this 'in the manner of the word', e.g. sing slowly.

■ Guesses have to be written on a board, one mark for every one correctly spelt; five extra marks for guessing the adverb. Donate a mark to every other classmate for incorrect spellings!

Prefixes and suffixes

Objective for Additional Unit 1

To use root words, prefixes and suffixes as support for spelling

Part 1 | You need

OHT A1; three different-coloured pens; dry-wipe boards or notebooks; Pupil's Book pages 38–39; PCM A1

Whole class
- Focus on the top half of the OHT and read the list of words together.
- Taking each word in turn, ask the children to identify any prefix or suffix and the word root, and underline these in the three different colours.
- Discuss the impact of the prefixes and suffixes and how they alter meaning, e.g. some prefixes create opposites.
- List other words with similar affixes, or take the root and use a different affix.
- Use the words from the OHT in sentences, e.g. *The insignificant ant carried out a nonsensical disappearing act. The misleading caterpillar had a disagreement with an unassuming python.*
- Introduce the oddbod: *sincerely* – see below.

Pupil activities
A: Add the prefix in to make opposites.
B: Remove prefixes to make opposites.
   (Note: *antisocial* becomes *social* and within the context of the sentence should be *sociable* – a possible discussion point. Tell children to look out for this catch-you-out.)
C: Add the prefixes il, im, in, ir to make opposites.

Think about…: Prefixes which create opposites.

Review
- Recap: prefixes and suffixes alter the meaning and function of words.
- Can children remind you which prefixes create opposites?

Homework
Investigate the spelling of prefixes and word roots when they are combined.

Oddbod   sincerely ②⬦
- Break the word into syllables and then spell each one separately.
- The first syllable sin is easy and the ending must be ly. So it is the middle syllable that may cause problems.
- Write up the whole word and underline the middle, cere. Children 'take a picture', then you cover the word and children speedwrite it.

Snip-snap   Break It Up! ②⊖〰
- Say a word and children break it into syllables, holding up the correct number of fingers. Then all chant the word together.
- Demonstrate how this helps to tackle words, by breaking them into manageable units, sometimes distinguishing roots, suffixes, prefixes.
- Try: *fol-low, up-stairs, ran-dom, un-fair, crum-pet, de-fend, rat-tle, dif-fe-rent, lem-on-ade, un-du-late, un-der-stand, max-i-mise, in-su-rance, car-pen-ter, rad-i-a-tor.*

NLS objective for Additional Unit 1

6.1.W5

Part 2 | **You need**   OHT A1; dry-wipe boards or notebooks

Whole class
- Summarise the rule that was covered in the homework activity: when prefixes are added on, generally the spelling of the prefix does not change. Note however, that al is used as a prefix, not all.
- Focus on the bottom half of the OHT and read through the clusters of words on the aliens.
- Ask children to match the correct prefix or suffix to each word cluster.
- Get Up and Go: ask volunteers to list other words that use the same prefix or suffix.
- Write some silly sentences, e.g. *The microscopic leadership tried to educate the aqueduct. The unusual friendship between an automobile driver and an emu was unnecessary and unkind.*

Review
- Ask children to recap the rule from the homework activity.
- Remind them that breaking words into syllables can aid spelling.

- Homework review.
- Check that children have found the exception: that we use al as a prefix, not all.

Follow-up homework
- Make sure that pupils are certain about the al rule. Encourage them to break words up into manageable chunks and look for affixes when spelling.

Test dictation
OB   The audience's laughter showed they had sincerely enjoyed the show.
A   I would never be champion because of my inability to run quickly.
     The bus is indirect so it is not very convenient.
B   The catalogue showed that the computer had been discontinued.
     The debate ended in argument and disagreement.
C   We were hoping for an improvement in the weather before sports day.

Snip-snap   Roots

- Divide the class into two teams. Write the following words on the board: *employment, improvement, punishment, agreement, amazement, commandment, assignment, argument, amusement, involvement, government, excitement.*
- Teams race to find and correctly write the base words, and to spot the odd one out.
- Score one point for each correctly spelt base word and a bonus to anyone who can explain why *argument* is the odd one out (it loses an e; the others just add the suffix straight onto the root word).

Snip-snap   Odd Plurals

- Say a singular word and children jot down the plural on dry-wipe boards. Try: *fish, tooth, goose, child, ox, mink, mouse, die, man, cherub, scissors, pants, sheep, lice, trousers, foot, deer, woman.*
- Point out that the word *children* shares the same plural pattern as *brethren*, and that some words, e.g. *scissors, trousers* and *pants*, have no singular forms.

Part 1

You need OHT A2, dry-wipe boards or notebooks; Pupil's Book pages 40–41; PCM A2

Whole class

- Focus on the top half of the OHT and read the words together.
- Ask the children to complete the 'How to remember' column. Make sure that all the different spelling strategies are used (see Review below).
- Show Me: choose words at random for children to write on dry-wipe boards.
- Use some of the words in sentences, e.g. *An argument broke out in the queue for chocolate cake but ended in a peaceful conclusion.*
- Introduce the oddbod: *sequence* – see below.

Pupil activities

A: Work out ways to remember spellings of easily confused words.
B: Identify relationships between words (spelling patterns, sounds, word roots).
C: Fill in the missing vowels. (Answers: *telephone, binoculars, question, portable, zoology, decision, biology*)

Extra challenge: Find words by filling in the missing consonants.

Review

- Look at the Extra challenge activity as a class. Remind children that it is important to use a range of strategies to help remember and learn spellings. These could include sounding the word out; breaking it into syllables; looking for an affix; looking for a root; finding relationship to another word by meaning, rhyme, sound or spelling pattern; using a rule or convention; using visual memory ('taking a picture'); using a mnemonic of some sort.

Homework

Find words in a wordsearch and identify the common pattern. Answers: *ocean, session, physician, Asian, optician, potion, motion, intuition, fiction, nation*; all end in shun.

Oddbod sequence

- Refer back to *consequence* in Unit 17.
- se has only one e.
- q must be followed by u.
- quen rhymes with *men*.
- Ending ce is the same as in *consequence*.
- Learn as a double: *sequences have consequences.*

Snip-snap Compounds

- Write up two lists of words and ask children to use them to create compound words, writing them on dry-wipe boards.
- It is vital that the words are joined – the word is incorrectly spelt unless they are joined and written as one word. (In tests such as the annual national tests this would be counted as an error.)
- Try: list 1: *net, foot, air, black, down, farm, wood, grape, card, on, up, out, in*; list 2: *ward, fruit, ball, house, craft, work, berry, board.*

NLS objectives for Additional Unit 2

6.3.W2   6.3.W3   6.3.W4

Part 2 | **You need**   OHT A2; dry-wipe boards or notebooks

Whole class
- Focus on the bottom half of the OHT and read the words together.
- Complete the 'How to remember' column by asking pupils how they can remember the spelling. Make sure that many different spelling strategies are used (see Part 1).
- Use some of the words in sentences, e.g. *My skilful friend advised me to beware the consequences of the outrageous questionnaire.*

Review
- Refer to the icons on the inside back cover of the Pupil's Book and discuss which senses might be useful when learning particular words on the OHT list.
- Ask children to remind you of any spelling rules for making plurals, e.g.
  - Many words just add s.
  - Words that end in y – change the y to i and add es (*babies*), unless the final letter is preceded by a vowel (*days*).
  - Some words that end in f or fe – change the f to v and add es (*thieves, knives*); others just add s (*chiefs*); words that end in ff – always just add s (*cliffs*).
  - Words that end in a shushing/hissing/buzzing sound – add es (*foxes*).
- Homework review.
- In pairs, children compare the words they found in the wordsearch and discuss how they were related to each other.

Follow-up homework
- Revisit any spelling rules that pupils are uncertain about – these need to be noted and reinforced.

Test dictation
OB It's important to do your homework in a logical sequence.
A   The astronaut was glad to get back to Earth.
    There is only one antidote for the snake's bite.
B   I clumsily dropped my portable television.
    There is a radar aboard every submarine.
C   I spotted the young lioness through my binoculars.

Snip-snap   Plurals ⊙ ⊚ ⊜ ⌣ ⊝
- Say a sentence with a plural word in it and children write the plural down on dry-wipe boards.
- Try sentences including the following: *apples, roads, stars, enemies, stories, parties, categories, misses, foxes, churches, buses, relays, donkeys, knees, elves, thieves, loaves, leaves, tomatoes.*
- Ask children to summarise the rules (see Review).

Snip-snap   Adding ed and ing ⊚
- Say a word and children write it on dry-wipe boards adding ed and ing, e.g. *stop – stopping – stopped.*
- Ask children to summarise the rule (see Review).
- Try: *clap, snap, plan, skip, trap, shut, sip, drag, nap.*

<table>
<tr><td colspan="2">Objective for Additional Unit 3</td></tr>
</table>

Objective for Additional Unit 3

To further develop an interest in spelling by manipulating letters, using knowledge of spelling rules and morphology

| **Part 1** | **You need** | OHT A3; dry-wipe boards or notebooks; Pupil's Book pages 42–43; PCM A3 |

Whole class
- Focus on the top half of the OHT and read the riddle together.
- Discuss how the riddle works: the clues refer to letters contained in the underlined words – a process of elimination until only one letter is left.
- Show Me: children work individually or in pairs and write the answer on dry-wipe boards. Some children might need a hint, e.g. it's a wild animal (answer: tiger).
- Invent a riddle together, e.g. *My first is in cook but not in book. / My second is in happy and also in sad. / My last is in track but not in crack.* (answer: *cat*)
- You might want to challenge more able pupils to use a rhyming pattern.
- Introduce the oddbod *encyclopedia* – see below.

Pupil activities
A and B: Write riddles.
C: Write acrostics.

Extra challenge: Write rhyming riddles.

Review
- Remind children that any activity that focuses upon words, spelling and meaning can help develop spelling ability and can be great fun!

Homework
Do **Look Say Cover Write Check** with the Year 7 spelling list to discover which words are already known.

Oddbod   encyclopedia
- Explain that an encyclopedia can be in book or CD-Rom form.
- Break the word into parts. (It can be spelt with either ae or just e in the middle.)
- Speedwrite pedia to get the feel of that part of the word.
- Write up the whole word, children 'take a picture' and chant, then cover it and children write it on dry-wipe boards.

Snip-snap   Reveal/Which One?
- Reveal: think of a word and write up the first letter only. Children write on boards what they think the word might be. You then write another letter, and so on until the word is correctly spelt.
- Which One?: write up several options for spelling a word. Children decide which is correct and then explain how they know – or how they can remember the spelling.

NLS objective for Additional Unit 3
6.3.W6

Part 2 | **You need**   OHT A3; dry-wipe boards or notebooks

Whole class
- Focus on the bottom half of the OHT and read the poem together.
- Take each line in turn and ask the children to explain how it is written. Note how each sentence plays on the saint's name, e.g. *stale – flat* and *ale – beer*.
- Use the words at the bottom to invent further lines – children record them on their dry-wipe boards.

Review
- Explain that playing with riddles and any other word game helps to further an investigative approach to spelling words, their meanings and patterns. Tell children that this will really help them in their Year 7 studies.

- Homework review.
- Keep the spelling list for Year 7 and during the holidays, begin to use your spelling strategies to learn some of the words.

Follow-up homework
- Children work in pairs and compare their invented lines.

Test dictation
OB An encyclopedia has facts about history, literature, geography and biology.
A   The ark had a pair of every kind of animal.
    The stray kitten was grateful to have found a home.
B   If you have a query, your teacher can often help.
    My brother has a ginger stripe in his fringe.
C   My uncle tells strange stories about ghosts in the cathedral.

Snip-snap   I Spy

- You could play this game in the usual way with letters. Alternatively, play it with sounds and start by saying, 'I spy with my little eye something beginning with **sh**'. (Use the sound **sh** rather than the letters sh.)
- Children guess the word and write it on their dry-wipe boards. Only a correct spelling is acceptable.

Snip-snap   Dominoes

- One child begins by saying a word, e.g. *cats*. The next player has three seconds to think of a word that starts with the final letter of that word.
- A sample sequence might be: s*ilence* – e*lephant* – t*omorrow* – w*ater* – r*at* – t*errapin* – n*ewt*.

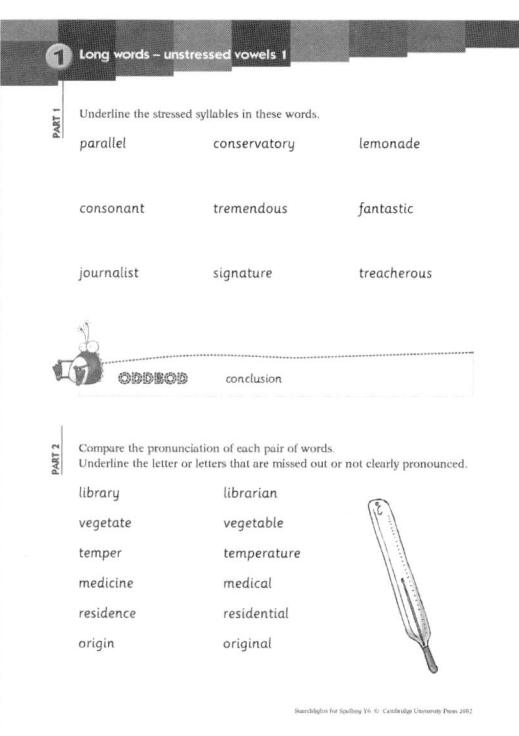

1 Long words – unstressed vowels 1

PART 1

Underline the stressed syllables in these words.

parallel   conservatory   lemonade

consonant   tremendous   fantastic

journalist   signature   treacherous

ODDBOD   conclusion

PART 2

Compare the pronunciation of each pair of words.
Underline the letter or letters that are missed out or not clearly pronounced.

library   librarian

vegetate   vegetable

temper   temperature

medicine   medical

residence   residential

origin   original

Searchlights for Spelling Y6 © Cambridge University Press 2002

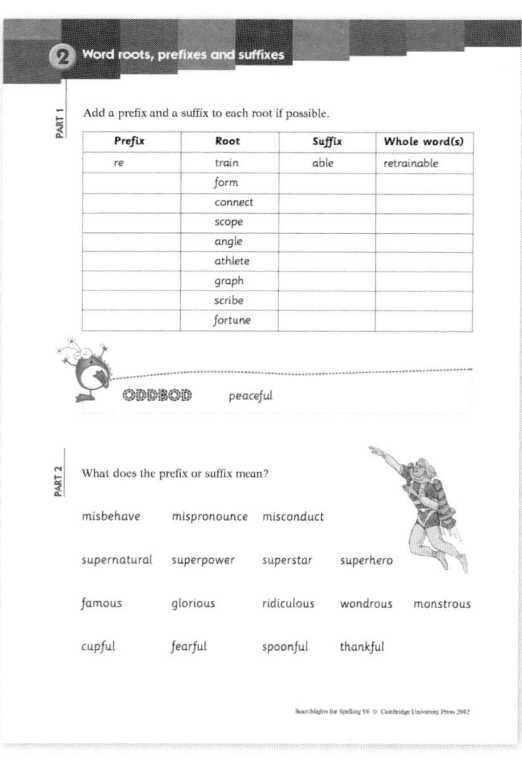

2 Word roots, prefixes and suffixes

PART 1

Add a prefix and a suffix to each root if possible.

Prefix	Root	Suffix	Whole word(s)
re	train	able	retrainable
	form		
	connect		
	scope		
	angle		
	athlete		
	graph		
	scribe		
	fortune		

ODDBOD   peaceful

PART 2

What does the prefix or suffix mean?

misbehave   mispronounce   misconduct

supernatural   superpower   superstar   superhero

famous   glorious   ridiculous   wondrous   monstrous

cupful   fearful   spoonful   thankful

Searchlights for Spelling Y6 © Cambridge University Press 2002

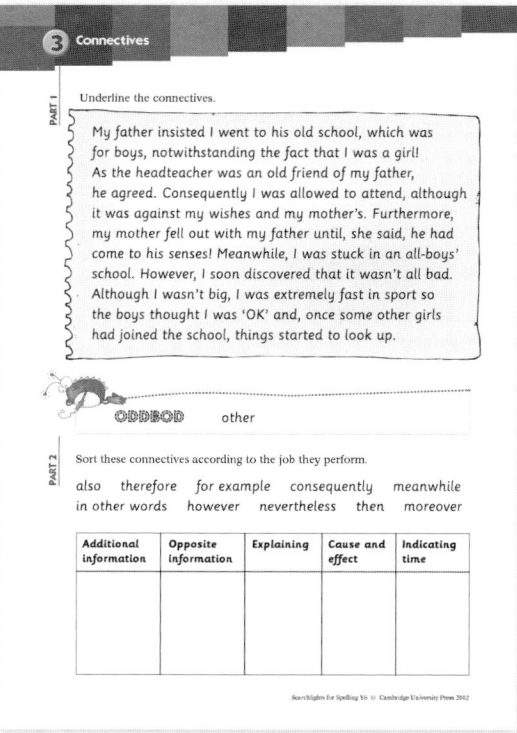

3 Connectives

PART 1

Underline the connectives.

My father insisted I went to his old school, which was
for boys, notwithstanding the fact that I was a girl!
As the headteacher was an old friend of my father,
he agreed. Consequently I was allowed to attend, although
it was against my wishes and my mother's. Furthermore,
my mother fell out with my father until, she said, he had
come to his senses! Meanwhile, I was stuck in an all-boys'
school. However, I soon discovered that it wasn't all bad.
Although I wasn't big, I was extremely fast in sport so
the boys thought I was 'OK' and, once some other girls
had joined the school, things started to look up.

ODDBOD   other

PART 2

Sort these connectives according to the job they perform.

also   therefore   for example   consequently   meanwhile
in other words   however   nevertheless   then   moreover

Additional information	Opposite information	Explaining	Cause and effect	Indicating time

Searchlights for Spelling Y6 © Cambridge University Press 2002

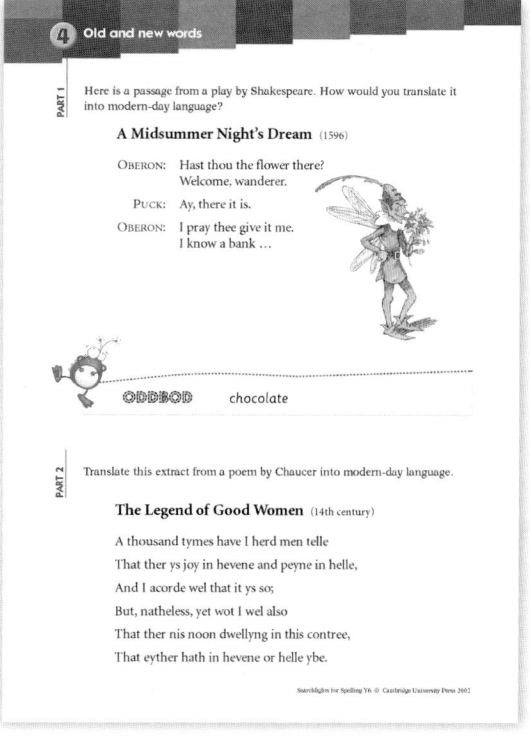

4 Old and new words

PART 1

Here is a passage from a play by Shakespeare. How would you translate it
into modern-day language?

A Midsummer Night's Dream (1596)

OBERON: Hast thou the flower there?
          Welcome, wanderer.

PUCK: Ay, there it is.

OBERON: I pray thee give it me.
          I know a bank …

ODDBOD   chocolate

PART 2

Translate this extract from a poem by Chaucer into modern-day language.

The Legend of Good Women (14th century)

A thousand tymes have I herd men telle

That ther ys joy in hevene and peyne in helle,

And I acorde wel that it ys so;

But, natheless, yet wot I wel also

That ther nis noon dwellyng in this contree,

That eyther hath in hevene or helle ybe.

Searchlights for Spelling Y6 © Cambridge University Press 2002

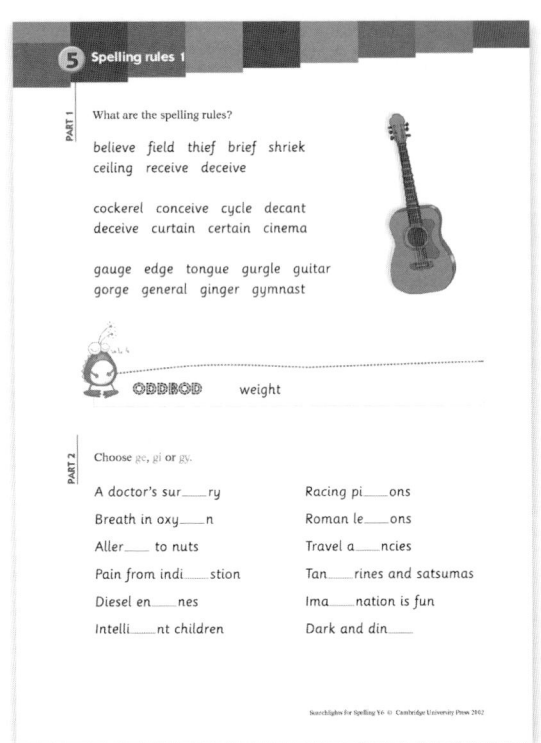

5 Spelling rules 1

PART 1

What are the spelling rules?

believe field thief brief shriek
ceiling receive deceive

cockerel conceive cycle decant
deceive curtain certain cinema

gauge edge tongue gurgle guitar
gorge general ginger gymnast

ODDBOD weight

PART 2

Choose *ge*, *gi* or *gy*.

A doctor's sur____ry   Racing pi____ons

Breath in oxy____n   Roman le____ons

Aller____ to nuts   Travel a____ncies

Pain from indi____stion   Tan____rines and satsumas

Diesel en____nes   Ima____nation is fun

Intelli____nt children   Dark and din____

Searchlights for Spelling Y6 © Cambridge University Press 2002

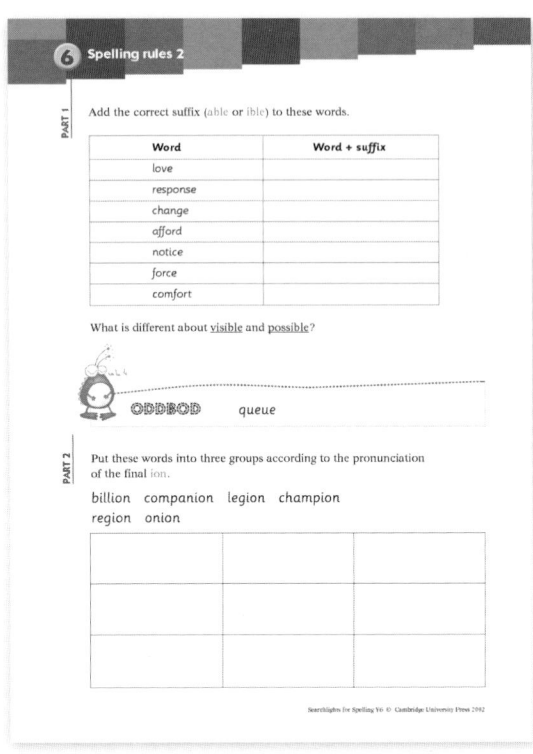

6 Spelling rules 2

PART 1

Add the correct suffix (*able* or *ible*) to these words.

Word	Word + suffix
love	
response	
change	
afford	
notice	
force	
comfort	

What is different about <u>visible</u> and <u>possible</u>?

ODDBOD queue

PART 2

Put these words into three groups according to the pronunciation of the final *ion*.

billion companion legion champion
region onion

Searchlights for Spelling Y6 © Cambridge University Press 2002

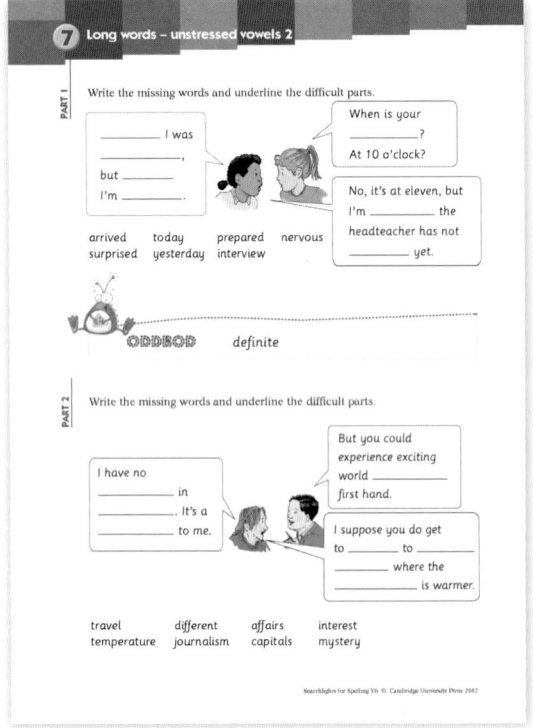

7 Long words – unstressed vowels 2

PART 1

Write the missing words and underline the difficult parts.

_____ I was _____,
but _____
I'm _____.

When is your _____?
At 10 o'clock?

No, it's at eleven, but I'm _____ the headteacher has not _____ yet.

arrived   today   prepared   nervous
surprised yesterday interview

ODDBOD definite

PART 2

Write the missing words and underline the difficult parts.

I have no _____ in _____. It's a _____ to me.

But you could experience exciting _____ world _____ first hand.

I suppose you do get to _____ to _____ where the _____ is warmer.

travel   different   affairs   interest
temperature journalism capitals   mystery

Searchlights for Spelling Y6 © Cambridge University Press 2002

---

8 Words for argument

PART 1

Root word	Related words
agree	agreement, disagree
argue	
belief	
conclude	
convince	
debate	
discuss	
reason	
sides	
state	
thought	

ODDBOD argument

PART 2

In an argument, which words from Part 1 would you use and when?

Introduction	One view	Opposing view	Conclusion

Searchlights for Spelling Y6 © Cambridge University Press 2002

Facsimile OHTs cont.

53

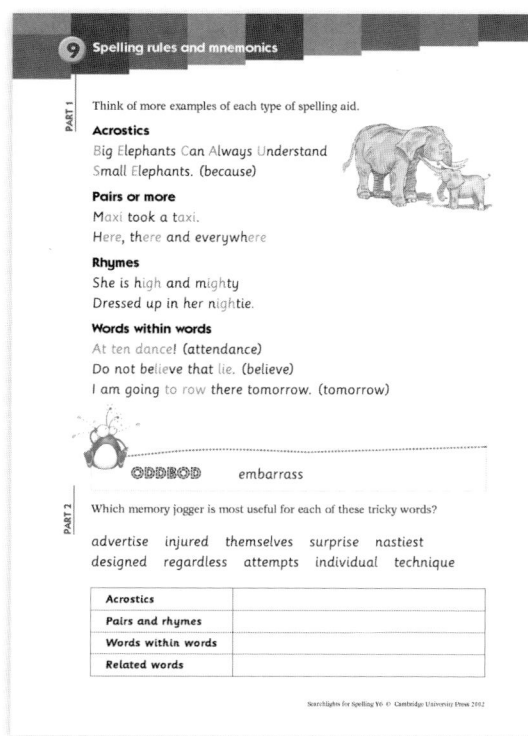

9 Spelling rules and mnemonics

PART 1

Think of more examples of each type of spelling aid.

Acrostics

Big Elephants Can Always Understand
Small Elephants. (because)

Pairs or more

Maxi took a taxi.
Here, there and everywhere

Rhymes

She is high and mighty
Dressed up in her nightie.

Words within words

At ten dance! (attendance)
Do not believe that lie. (believe)
I am going to row there tomorrow. (tomorrow)

ODDBOD   embarrass

PART 2

Which memory jogger is most useful for each of these tricky words?

advertise   injured   themselves   surprise   nastiest
designed   regardless   attempts   individual   technique

Acrostics	
Pairs and rhymes	
Words within words	
Related words	

Searchlights for Spelling Y6 © Cambridge University Press 2002

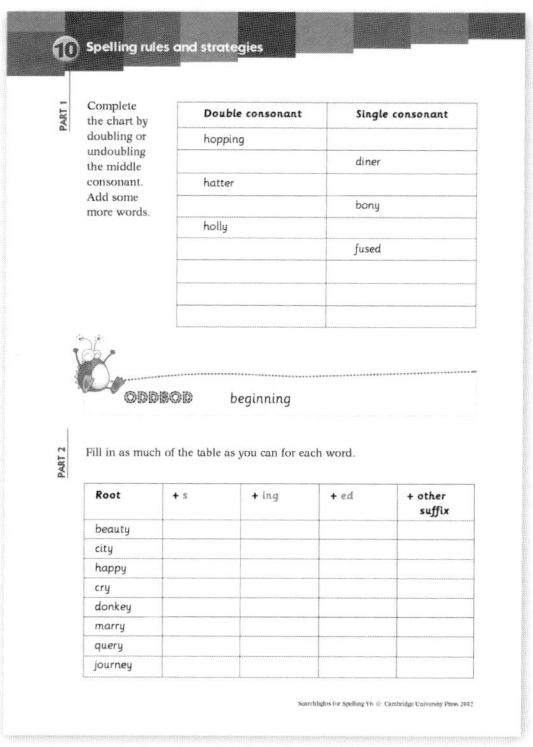

10 Spelling rules and strategies

PART 1

Complete the chart by doubling or undoubling the middle consonant. Add some more words.

Double consonant	Single consonant
hopping	
	diner
hatter	
	bony
holly	
	fused

ODDBOD   beginning

PART 2

Fill in as much of the table as you can for each word.

Root	+ s	+ ing	+ ed	+ other suffix
beauty				
city				
happy				
cry				
donkey				
marry				
query				
journey				

Searchlights for Spelling Y6 © Cambridge University Press 2002

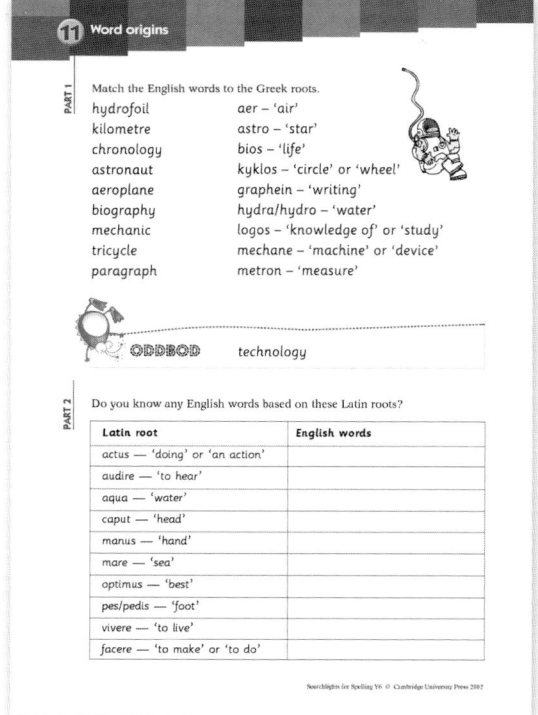

11 Word origins

PART 1

Match the English words to the Greek roots.

hydrofoil   aer – 'air'
kilometre   astro – 'star'
chronology   bios – 'life'
astronaut   kyklos – 'circle' or 'wheel'
aeroplane   graphein – 'writing'
biography   hydra/hydro – 'water'
mechanic   logos – 'knowledge of' or 'study'
tricycle   mechane – 'machine' or 'device'
paragraph   metron – 'measure'

ODDBOD   technology

PART 2

Do you know any English words based on these Latin roots?

Latin root	English words
actus — 'doing' or 'an action'	
audire — 'to hear'	
aqua — 'water'	
caput — 'head'	
manus — 'hand'	
mare — 'sea'	
optimus — 'best'	
pes/pedis — 'foot'	
vivere — 'to live'	
facere — 'to make' or 'to do'	

Searchlights for Spelling Y6 © Cambridge University Press 2002

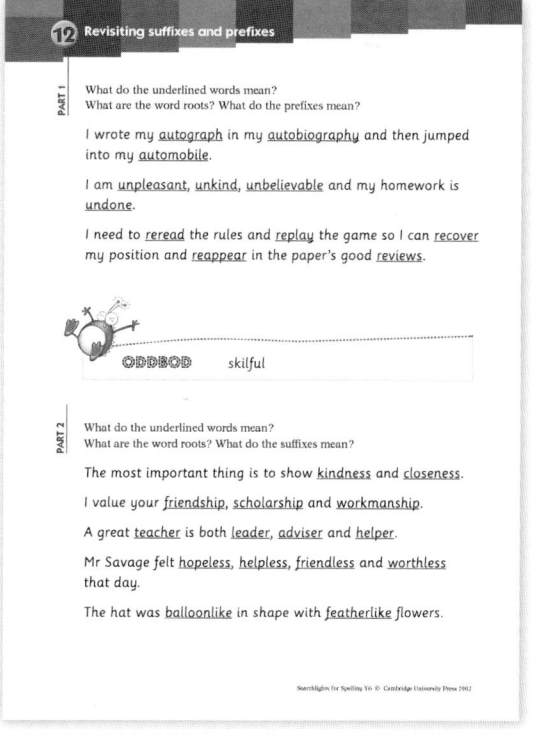

12 Revisiting suffixes and prefixes

PART 1

What do the underlined words mean?
What are the word roots? What do the prefixes mean?

I wrote my autograph in my autobiography and then jumped into my automobile.

I am unpleasant, unkind, unbelievable and my homework is undone.

I need to reread the rules and replay the game so I can recover my position and reappear in the paper's good reviews.

ODDBOD   skilful

PART 2

What do the underlined words mean?
What are the word roots? What do the suffixes mean?

The most important thing is to show kindness and closeness.

I value your friendship, scholarship and workmanship.

A great teacher is both leader, adviser and helper.

Mr Savage felt hopeless, helpless, friendless and worthless that day.

The hat was balloonlike in shape with featherlike flowers.

Searchlights for Spelling Y6 © Cambridge University Press 2002

54

13 Confusables

PART 1

Which words sound the same?

quay	stationery
practise	serial
aloud	principal
which	key
threw	through
cereal	practice
principle	past
passed	allowed
stationary	witch

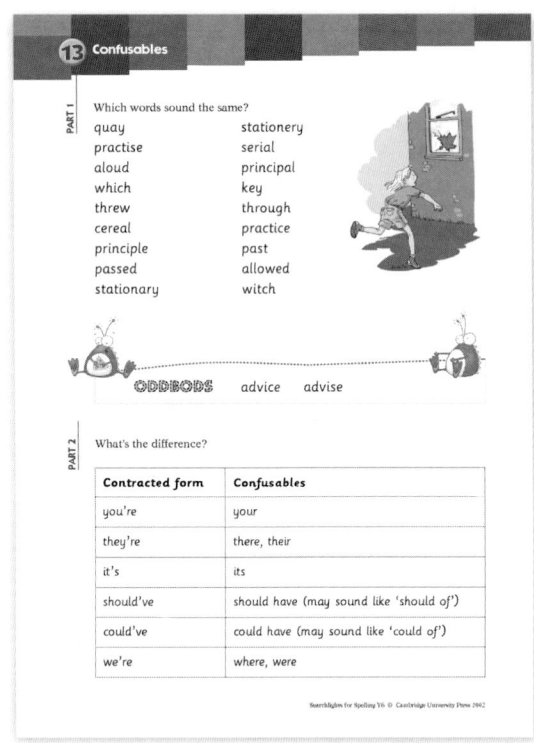

ODDBODS   advice   advise

PART 2

What's the difference?

Contracted form	Confusables
you're	your
they're	there, their
it's	its
should've	should have (may sound like 'should of')
could've	could have (may sound like 'could of')
we're	where, were

Searchlights for Spelling Y6 © Cambridge University Press 2002

14 Spelling rules and strategies 2

PART 1

A Midsummer Night's Dream (1596)

TITANIA: Be kind and courteous to this gentleman;
Hop in his walks and gambol in his eyes;
Feed him with apricots and dewberries,
With purple grapes, green figs and mulberries;
The honey bags steal from the humble-bees, . . .

Find the words with 'long' vowel phonemes. Sort them according to their sound.

ai		ie	
oa		oo	
ee			

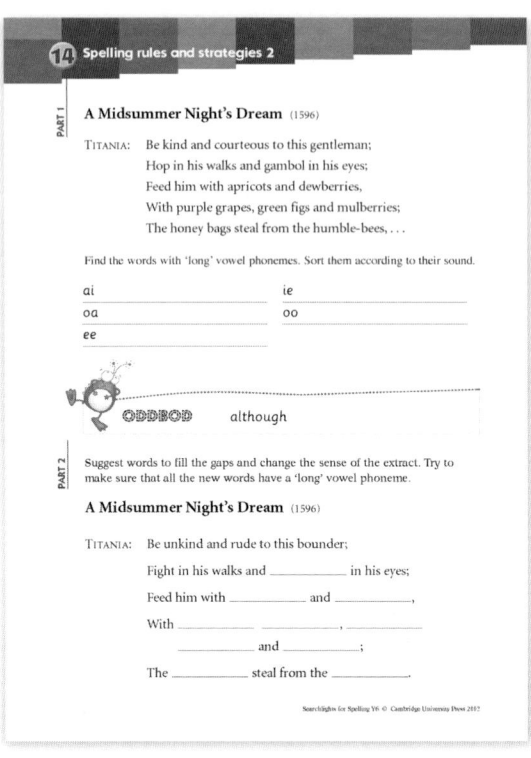

ODDBOD   although

PART 2

Suggest words to fill the gaps and change the sense of the extract. Try to make sure that all the new words have a 'long' vowel phoneme.

A Midsummer Night's Dream (1596)

TITANIA: Be unkind and rude to this bounder;

Fight in his walks and _____ in his eyes;

Feed him with _____ and _____,

With _____ _____, _____,

_____ and _____;

The _____ steal from the _____.

Searchlights for Spelling Y6 © Cambridge University Press 2002

15 Spelling of dialect and memory joggers

PART 1

Rewrite the text using conventional spellings.

Biby's Epitaph

A muvver was barfin' 'er biby one night,
The youngest of ten and a tiny young mite,
The muvver was poor and the biby was thin,
Only a skelington covered in skin;
The muvver turnd rahnd for the soap off the rack,
She was but a moment, but when she turned back,
The biby was gorn; and in anguish she cried,
'Oh, where is my biby?' – the angels replied . . .

Anon.

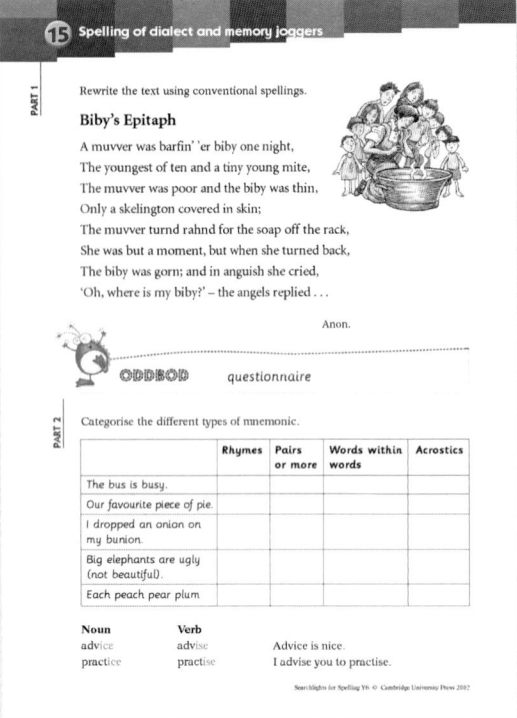

ODDBOD   questionnaire

PART 2

Categorise the different types of mnemonic.

	Rhymes	Pairs or more	Words within words	Acrostics
The bus is busy.				
Our favourite piece of pie.				
I dropped an onion on my bunion.				
Big elephants are ugly (not beautiful).				
Each peach pear plum				

Noun	Verb	
advice	advise	Advice is nice.
practice	practise	I advise you to practise.

Searchlights for Spelling Y6 © Cambridge University Press 2002

16 Sound and spelling patterns plus silent letters

PART 1

How are the words in each list similar to each other?

bought	bough	back
caught	through	black
court	cough	clack
fort	tough	crack
taught	although	flack
quart	thorough	hack
taut		jack
wart		lack
		knack
		pack

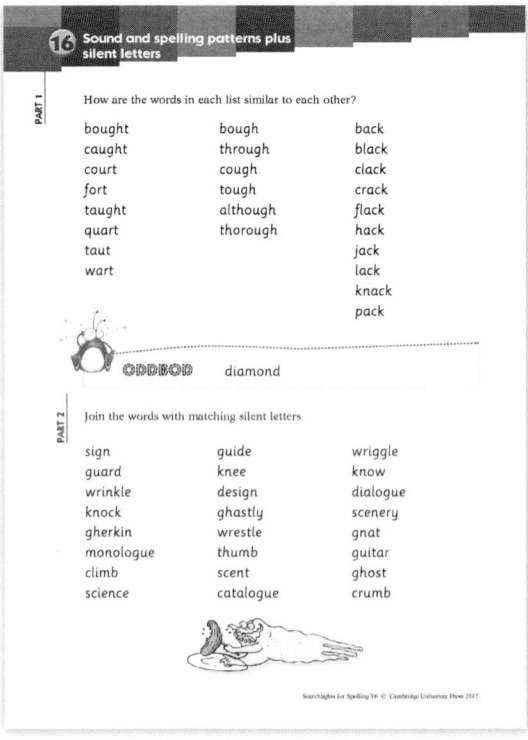

ODDBOD   diamond

PART 2

Join the words with matching silent letters.

sign	guide	wriggle
guard	knee	know
wrinkle	design	dialogue
knock	ghastly	scenery
gherkin	wrestle	gnat
monologue	thumb	guitar
climb	scent	ghost
science	catalogue	crumb

Searchlights for Spelling Y6 © Cambridge University Press 2002

17 Word play

Where do witches go to learn?	Spelling classes!
What is the plural of mouse?	Mice!
What is the plural of house?	Hice!
What is the plural of baby?	Twins!
Give me a sentence with the word politics in it.	Our parrot swallowed the alarm clock and now poli-tics!
Please Miss, I've swallowed my pencil sharpener. No Miss, I'm perfectly serious!	You must be choking!
What do you get if you look at a vampire teacher through a telescope?	A horror-scope!
Where do skinny teachers train?	At puny-versity!

ODDBOD   consequence

PART 2

Look at these spoonerisms. Correct each sentence.

He's a boiled sprat.
Let me sew you to a sheet.
You have tasted a whole worm.

Spoonerise these words.

packed lunch
letter-box
rounders bat

Searchlights for Spelling Y6 © Cambridge University Press 2012

18 Word games

PART 1

Underline the letters used to make the new words.

Poerse

I saw a cat sleaming on a chair,	sleeping/dreaming
I saw a rabbit snaped in the glare,	snared/trapped
I saw a car scrushing down the road,	rushing/screeching
I saw a man larrying a load,	carrying/lifting
I saw a boy shelling at the sky,	shouting/yelling
I saw a baker grobble up pie,	gobble/greedy
I saw a rocket swooming in space,	zooming/swiftly
I saw a tailor clewing with lace,	sewing/clumsily
I saw a Mum siddling her baby,	singing to/cuddling
And maybe, maybe I saw you too.	

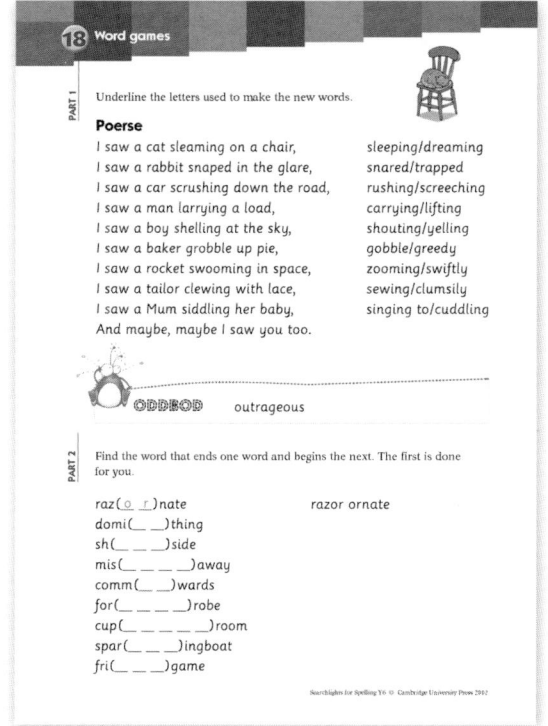

ODDBOD   outrageous

PART 2

Find the word that ends one word and begins the next. The first is done for you.

raz(o r)nate   razor ornate
domi(_ _)thing
sh(_ _ _)side
mis(_ _ _ _)away
comm(_ _)wards
for(_ _ _ _)robe
cup(_ _ _ _)room
spar(_ _ _)ingboat
fri(_ _ _)game

Searchlights for Spelling Y6 © Cambridge University Press 2012

Additional Unit 1: Prefixes and suffixes

PART 1

Identify the prefixes, suffixes and word roots.

insignificant	immigration	unhappiness	unassuming
nonsensical	undoing	discontinued	misleading
disappearing	supervision	immobilisation	disagreement

ODDBOD   sincerely

PART 2

Write the correct prefix or suffix to match each alien to its pet.

micro   auto   trans   ship   un   over

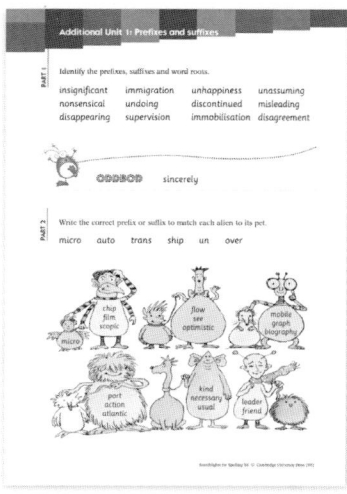

Searchlights for Spelling Y6 © Cambridge University Press 2012

Additional Unit 2: Spelling strategies and common words

PART 1

Make a note of how to remember these spellings.

Difficult words	How to remember spelling
other	There is a *her* in other.
peaceful	
conclusion	
chocolate	
weight	
queue	
definite	
argument	
embarrass	
beginning	

ODDBOD   sequence

PART 2

Make a note of how to remember these spellings.

Difficult words	How to remember spelling
outrageous	Words within the word: *oat*, *rag*
technology	
skilful	
although	
questionnaire	
diamond	
consequence	
sincerely	
encyclopedia	
advise	

Searchlights for Spelling Y6 © Cambridge University Press 2012

Additional Unit 3: Word play and spelling check-up

PART 1

Solve the clues to find each letter of the answer.

Riddle

My first is in <u>foot</u> and also in <u>print</u>.
My second is in <u>height</u> but never in <u>length</u>.
My third is in <u>singing</u> but never in <u>noisy</u>.
My fourth is in <u>shoes</u> and also in <u>feet</u>.
My last is in <u>teacher</u> but never in <u>cheat</u>.
What creature am I?

ODDBOD   encyclopedia

PART 2

Saintly sentences

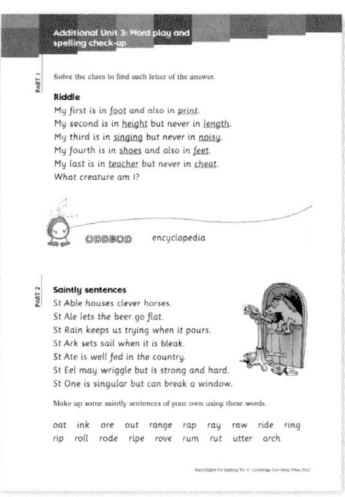

St Able houses clever horses.
St Ale lets the beer go flat.
St Rain keeps us trying when it pours.
St Ark sets sail when it is bleak.
St Ate is well fed in the country.
St Eel may wriggle but is strong and hard.
St One is singular but can break a window.

Make up some saintly sentences of your own using these words.

oat ink are out range rap ray raw ride ring
rip roll rode ripe rove rum rut utter arch

Searchlights for Spelling Y6 © Cambridge University Press 2012